Jerry B. Jenkins

AS YOU

LEAVE

HOME

Parting thoughts from a loving parent

Colorado Springs, Colorado

AS YOU LEAVE HOME
Copyright © 1993 by Jerry B. Jenkins
The author is represented by the literary agency of Alive Communications, P.O. Box 49068, Colorado Springs, Colorado 80949.

Library of Congress Cataloging-in-Publication Data
Jenkins, Jerry B.
    As you leave home: parting thoughts from a loving parent / Jerry B. Jenkins
        p. cm.
    Includes bibliographical references.
    ISBN 1-56179-132-6
    1. Young adults—United States—Life skills guides. 2. Young adults—United States—
        Religious life. I. Title.
    HQ799.7.J45 1993
    305.23'5—dc20   92-33485
                                     CIP

Published by Focus on the Family Publishing, Colorado Springs, Colorado 80995.
Distributed in the U.S. and Canada by Word Books, Dallas, Texas.
Scripture quotations are from THE NEW KING JAMES VERSION of the Bible. Copyright © 1979, 1980, 1982, Thomas Nelson, Inc., Publishers.
Some people's names and certain details of stories mentioned in this book have been changed to protect the privacy of the individuals involved.
Editor: Larry K. Weeden
Designer: Jeff Stoddard
Printed in the United States of America
93 94 95 96 97/10 9 8 7 6 5 4 3 2

for Dallas

contents

PART ONE

just between us

one. nothing can tear us apart

And so it has come down to this: You're going. Really going. Oh, you'll be back. It isn't as if I will never see you again. But when you return, you'll come as a guest. For all practical purposes, you are gone for good.

Though you'll always remain in my heart and be a member of our family, nothing will be the same. While I may finance your life-style temporarily, you are now your own person, making your own decisions, disciplining or not disciplining yourself.

It's stunning to realize that the clichés are true. All those platitudes I heard last week, when you were born, are now indisputable. "Hang on to every moment, every day," I was told when I showed you off as our new arrival. "Before you know it, they'll be gone."

I nodded and smiled and pretended to agree, to know, to understand something beyond my wisdom. What did I know? I was barely more than a child myself, and the first couple of decades of my own life had seemed to plod along. Somehow, if everyone could be believed, the next two would take no more time than a turn of the head.

Now I tell new parents the same. I know. I mean it. I plead with them to heed, and they nod and smile and pretend to agree. Perhaps to them last night's diaper change made the wee hours (pun intended) seem eternal. How I long to be awakened and needed in such an innocent way now! New parents wonder if those tedious times ever end, and tomorrow they'll wonder where they went.

You're at an age when you don't want to be told what you do and don't understand. So forgive the lump in my throat, the catch in my voice, and the glaze in my eye. *They were right! They were right!* is all I can think. You were here such a short time, and if I had my way, I would hold you desperately and keep you here.

How surprising that must sound. I know. I was there once. I remember when getting out was a consuming passion. When it seemed the feeling was mutual. Why, then, my loved ones' emotion, the tears, the nostalgia at my leaving?

Much as you don't want to hear it and perhaps don't even want to think about it, the fact is you can't understand me just now. You will. Your own child will educate you beyond any classroom or degree. You'll cradle that baby in your arms, and anything else you ever cared about will pale to worthlessness. Your life, your being will focus on that child. Though you'll know and be reminded by experts that it's not healthy to center your existence on your child, you will do it anyway, helplessly. You'll be awash in a kind of love not often expressed articulately, because there are so few words for it.

Then, too, there are so many distractions to the communication of that love. As you think back to your years at home, you may think of difficult times, of frustration, of quarreling, misunderstanding, lack of connecting. My years—here I go again—allow me to see those as only part of the whole, bits of a beautiful mosaic, the underside of an embroidered fabric.

I love you with all that is within me, with a love beyond words. It may take weeks, even months, to adjust to your absence. But even when I have overcome that and adapted to a freedom that long sounded attractive, some things will never change. You need to know that.

As you grew, you heard me say silly things like, "Where was I when you were getting so tall?" "Since when did you become so good looking?" "How could you be a teenager already? Weren't you just in first grade?"

You shake your head and wonder how adults can be so nerdy. I once felt the same. Yet now, in earnest passion, I try to convince you that life is, indeed, short. It *is* a vapor that appears for an instant and then vanishes.[1]

Watching you as a freshman, I wondered what your mature body would be like when you were a senior. Suddenly the sophomore and junior years blipped past my radar screen, and I didn't have to wonder. There you were, mature and defined, on the move. I tried to let go as I longed to hang on, so forgive me if the parting has come too quickly.

The songwriter tried to tell us in her beautiful lyric that the moment we try to hold in our hands slips through our fingers like sand. "Yesterday's gone, and tomorrow may never come, but we have this moment today. . . . Hold them near while they're here and don't wait for tomorrow to look back and wish for today."[2]

I heard that message and was moved by it, and I even tried to heed it. But I didn't know how true it was until now. My hands are open and reaching, and the sand is gone. The moment is past. You're leaving.

Much as I knew that preparing you for this day was a priority, I spent less time preparing myself. But I don't want you focused—especially now—on my melancholy, because I am proud. I am hopeful. I am praying. I want only the best for you; that's what love is.

Only my selfishness would tell me I'd rather have you stay than go. That's the same selfishness that is jealous of heaven when a beloved saint is taken. That covetousness would cup a butterfly in our palms and withhold it from its purpose, its freedom.

So as you think about me with whatever emotion is appropriate, feel free to not focus on my pain, my longing—yes, my grief. It's a hurdle. It's my burden, not yours. I inform you of it for a higher purpose: to let you know the depth of my love for you.

I know you'll make me proud, because you already have. At this transition, you need to know only one truth. It was best expressed by the same lyricist as above when she wrote:

We'd like to collect you and shield and protect you
And save you from hurts if we could;
But we must let you grow tall, to learn and to know all
That God has in mind for your good.
We never could own you, for God only loaned you

To widen our world and our hearts.
So, we wish you His freedom, knowing where He is leading,
There is nothing can tear us apart.[3]

Though there are many things you could do, out there on your own, to disappoint me, hurt me, or even repulse me, nothing can tear us apart. You might even take actions or choose a life-style so nauseating to me that you would be unwelcome in my home as long as you persisted. In a worst-case scenario, I might choose not to finance, let alone condone, such behavior.

Yet like the father in the parable of the prodigal son, I will stand scanning the horizon for your return. Nothing you can ever do will make you other than my child. I will love you, cherish you, pray for you, and stand ready to forgive you. Anything else would mock the unconditional love God has bestowed on us by calling us His children, which He did even while we were dead in our sins:

"But God, who is rich in mercy, because of His great love with which He loved us, even when we were dead in trespasses, made us alive together with Christ (by grace you have been saved)."[4]

Today is a day when I wish I could approximate the unconditional love of God. Where I have failed to communicate that to you, I can only apologize and ask your forgiveness. For those times when you have felt that my pleasure in you, my love for you, my acceptance of you has been based on performance, I must take responsibility. I'm sorry.

And while I'm a finite, imperfect, sinful person myself, my goals are lofty. I want you to know and believe that your parents love you more than anything on earth. No matter what you do or don't do, say or don't say, start or don't start, finish or don't finish, accomplish or don't accomplish, you will still be my child. I will still love you.

You may be gone from our home, but you will never be gone from my heart. You may choose to leave so that you can cleave to someone else. That is one thing.

But nothing can tear us apart.

two. you always have a refuge
(but you're on your own)

during the last year or so, after I first realized that the rest of your life had inexplicably sped past, I tried not to be obvious. But maybe you noticed. In spite of myself, I tried to slow the calendar, stop the clock. I was trying, of course, to hang on to you.

The very thing I committed myself to years ago—rearing, raising, training you for independence—I now feared. I scrambled, shored up, built walls. Every sign that indicated you had learned and matured and were ready to face the world only reminded me how young you seemed.

But I couldn't run from the truth. You were leaving, and the day was coming soon. I was almost so desperate to hang on that I couldn't even exult in your growth and progress. That maddening independence, that I-can-do-it-myself attitude that reminded me so much of toddlerhood, that look that asked "Why do you have to know everything?" or "What does it matter to you?" should have cemented in my aching heart the truth: You had become your own person.

It's what I had wanted. I just hadn't wanted it this quickly. There are days when I don't want it at all. Yet I know this is for the best. It's time. And from my perspective, there will never be a good time. But I am committed to keeping my selfishness at bay. I will, I must, stop pretending that the longer I hang on to you, the more I protect you from the real world. If you don't jump in, you'll never find yourself. And so I nudge you from the nest.

Seeing you go reminds me of the first time I let loose of you in the water. Only this time I am not going to be at arm's length, ready to grab as you panic. I will not stand by with reassuring words that say, "I'm just seeing if you can float alone." This is the real thing. I will let go, you will flail, and I will back away.

The other metaphor that comes to mind is your first time on two wheels. I ran along beside, reaching, adjusting, holding the seat, helping you gain momentum and speed. Soon you were on your wobbly way, unable to turn, riding through puddles, over curbs, slowing to painful, tumbling stops before leaping up to try again.

Now I will give your two-wheeler a last shove and watch. No more running alongside. You've had enough of that. You won't admit it, but there will be times, maybe many (secretly I hope for that), when you'll whirl around, expecting me to be there. I won't be, and you'll think twice about calling, about asking to be bailed out of a jam.

There will be bumps and bruises, much as I'd like to protect you from them. You will be swindled, ripped off, maybe even endangered because of your own naïveté. I could intervene, could warn you, could slow you on a headlong path to believing someone because he "seemed like such a great guy." I could urge you to let time be the test of relationships, to think twice, even three times, before investing in anything. But you must learn from your own mistakes.

I know, because I've been there. I've gone against my own better judgment, so why shouldn't you? I knew better, or should have. I had been told enough times. But some things you must learn on your own. Another cliché has sprung to life: Experience is the best teacher.

You'll fail, and you'll kick yourself and wonder why you forged ahead. But some day you'll know that your life was shaped by the lessons you could learn only from your own mistakes.

Now let me be firm, just one last time. Against all emotion and that infuriating drive I have to collect you, to shield and protect you (as the Gaither song says), I know better. I know I would be doing you the greatest disservice of all to deprive you of life's own education.

If birds didn't push their awkward offspring from the nest and force them to flap and flutter to keep from slamming to the ground, the babies would grow fat and immobile in the nest. When it came time to migrate, they would be left behind. Protected from the danger of early flight, they would have been sentenced to die from inertia.

It may be my own insecurity, a lack of confidence in my influence over you, that will make me worry about you. Out of sight and out of mind, I'll wonder if you remember every bit of advice, every warning. How will I know whether I've shaped you at all? Maybe I've done nothing but make you want to run from my counsel and training. My worst nightmare is that you can't wait to get out from under my authority and try everything I ever prohibited you from doing. Or maybe I simply have too good a memory of my own emotions at your age.

Only now can I understand why parents see themselves in the parable of the prodigal son. I see in you tendencies toward selfishness, impudence, and wastefulness. Why? Because those tendencies are in me, too. And rather than dwelling on your wonderful qualities as I should, what will stick in my mind while worrying about you are negative memories. Yes, there are a few, and while there may have been many more major than these trifles, it's direction that concerns me.

When at four you ate all the frosting off the cupcake and then didn't want the rest, you had yet to learn the necessity of delayed gratification. When at eight you didn't ration out your gum and stuffed all the pieces in your mouth at once, and when at 14 you played before you worked and then didn't have time to work, you were merely acting your age. In my weak moments, I will remember that and picture you in pig slop with the biblical bad boy who broke his father's heart.

What I should do, of course, is remember those times when you were generous, when you gave of yourself, when you sacrificed, when you showed a spark of the divine. For that I would like to take credit, too, but in my fear and timidity I will be forced to attribute those qualities to the God who saved you. I will not make the mistake of ascribing to you some innate goodness apart from Him, and my prayer is that I will merely be able to have confidence in your decision-making wisdom.

I have urged you to never be a quitter, to never give up, to stay at the task even when the outlook is bleak. Now I want to clarify that this means you are on your own. I have not abandoned you, but I have cut you loose. And just as it is important for me to let you go and make your own mistakes, so it is vital that you not see me or our home as a crutch. I am not a way station that would keep you from building your own muscle. My door is shut so you'll know I believe you can solve your own problems, find your own solutions, develop your own strategies.

I am, of course, still your friend, so if and when I can help you as a friend would, I am here. And when you need an ear, I'm here. When you need a loan—not a gift—if I am able, I'm here.

If it insults you that I feel the need to remind you that you are now on your own, forgive me. The second to the last thing I want you to picture in your mind is that the shut door I just mentioned is also locked. (The last is that I'm here to make your life easier.)

I make that careful distinction because the day may come when life defeats you. If you are injured or ill to the point that you can't function, I am still your parent, we are still your family. If you fail so miserably that your options are gone and you can't go on, by all means know that here, with me, you have a refuge.

You may be so bitterly disappointed or grieving that you simply need to know someone is behind you. Never doubt it. If you lose a spouse, a child, or a home, you are still part of this family. You may have left and cleaved to someone else, but you still have a refuge.

In case you're wondering how serious things have to become before you should look this way, try these on for size:

If your course load is too heavy, don't come running home.

If you have procrastinated to the point where you will fail no matter how hard you work, don't come running home.

If you have come to loggerheads with your spouse, and understanding and communication are gone, don't come running home.

Stay in the game. Work at it, study it, plan for it, pray it through. You're on your own. You're building muscle. You're becoming a person who will one day train another to become independent.

On the other hand, if you feel estranged from me, if you wonder whether I still care, if you doubt my arms are still open, look to the horizon. I have for years identified with the parent in that fabled parable, and I can grasp the joy of seeing the prodigal return. But imagine! If the father was elated, what must the son have felt?

Luke 15:20 says that "he arose and came to his father. But when he was still a great way off, his father saw him and had compassion, and ran and fell on his neck and kissed him."

Where must the father have been to see his son when the son was "still a great way off"? If the father could see the son, the son could see the father on the horizon. And when the father realized it was, indeed, the son, he ran to him.

If you return as a prodigal—defeated, grieving, mourning, ashamed, or needy—you have a refuge. But when you are tempted to see my open arms, my running to you, as alternatives to digging your nails into the gritty stuff of life and extracting your own solutions, you should rethink your course. I'm here as a last aid, not first aid. When what I have to offer would rescue you from the abyss, turn your heart toward home. When I would merely stunt your growth by keeping you from doing your independent duty—hard as it may be —keep your heart right there where it belongs.

There can be no substitute for your relationship with God. He is the one to turn to in advance of trouble. Oh, trouble will still find you. The Bible says man is born to trouble, as surely as sparks fly upward.[1] Yet the writer goes on, "But as for me, I would seek God, and to God I would commit my cause; Who does great things, and unsearchable, marvelous things without number."[2]

That's where I would have you turn in time of trouble as well as calm. As much as I love you, as much as I care, as willingly as I would offer all that I possess to fix whatever ails you, I am but a microcosm of what your heavenly Father has to offer.

If my helping now—when you should be on your own—would keep you from maturing, pointing you to Him who knows all things[3] can only be the best course. God knows when to act and when to wait far better than we earthly, finite ones who love you.

I care more than I can say and more than you can ever know (at least until you become a parent yourself). But my efforts and even my love pale in comparison to His. Do I care? A thousand times yes. Does Jesus care? Infinitely, eternally. In a poem by Frank E. Graeff, put to music by J. Lincoln Hall, this was beautifully expressed:

Does Jesus Care?[4]

Does Jesus care when my heart is pained
Too deeply for mirth and song—
As the burdens press, and the cares distress,
And the way grows weary and long?

Does Jesus care when my way is dark
With a nameless dread and fear?

As the daylight fades into deep night shades,
Does He care enough to be near?

Does Jesus care when I've tried and failed
To resist some temptation strong?
When for my deep grief I find no relief,
Tho my tears flow all the night long?

Does Jesus care when I've said good-bye
To the dearest on earth to me,
And my sad heart aches till it nearly breaks—
Is it aught to Him? does He see?

O yes, He cares — I know He cares!
His heart is touched with my grief;
When the days are weary, the long nights dreary,
I know my Savior cares.

PART TWO

somewhere out there

three. major on the majors

orgive me in advance for not being more profound, but the older I get, the simpler my philosophies become. There was a time when I found all the complexities of theology and denominational differences fascinating—worth studying, discussing, even arguing over. But if you haven't already wearied of when-you-get-to-be-my-age platitudes, let me try this one on you and hope it isn't banal:

Purists may excoriate me for this, but with certain obvious exceptions— the basic Christological doctrines of the New Testament, for instance—I've found myself growing more tolerant over the years. Denominational differences I now would rather call preferences, and the things I used to go to the mat over are now mere distinctives. I'm no longer willing to scrape a stick in the dirt and say, "You're on this side with me, or you're wrong."

That doesn't mean I have to (or ever will) be entirely comfortable with certain modes of worship, types of music, or faith practices. It does mean the time has long since come and gone when I feel I must separate from other followers of Christ over differences of opinion.

Of course, if someone wants to tell you that God is a chauvinist, that Jesus or the disciples were homosexuals, that all roads lead to God and one religion is as good as another,[1] or that Jesus wasn't God or didn't really rise from the dead, find your stick and draw your line.

But if someone who has trusted in Christ alone for salvation disagrees with you on how emotional to be in church, when Jesus is coming back, or whether drums are appropriate in the sanctuary, celebrate your diversity!

I'm not saying you shouldn't have opinions on these issues, or even that neither of you is right. If you're on opposite sides of an issue, someone has to be right. The point is that the older you get (here I go again), the more obvious it will become to you that these are not issues over which to part company. Few enough people believe in the exclusivity of the gospel as it is. Protect the relationships you have with those who do.

Major on the majors. Be careful about your view of Scripture. Those who would pick and choose what's truth and what's opinion, what's literal and what's figurative, what's fact and what's allegorical, can prove interesting and challenging. Without your head in the sand or your brain on hold, at some point you need to put your faith in the God of the Word and the Word of that God. We don't have to understand everything to accept that the message appears in those pages the way the Messenger wanted us to have it.

As you get out into the world, you'll see that despair reigns. Dig beneath the surface of any relationship and you'll find pain—painful memories, painful backgrounds, baggage that weighs down the best of them. You may have some of your own. When a friend's father is an alcoholic, when another's is abusive, when bankruptcy has struck another household, you'll see that the only constant is the need. And the need is for God.

The majors we must major on become fewer until they can be distilled to simple phrases. Of course, there's no such thing as a simple answer to a complex problem. But while my counsel is to avoid spouting platitudes for every situation, it does all boil down to Him, doesn't it?

Jesus loves you.

Jesus cares about you.

Jesus died for you.

Jesus is alive.

Jesus is coming again.

That's it. That's all there is. As I said, forgive me for not being more profound. And shame on me if I imply that simply saying the above will solve anything in anyone's life. Learning those truths and applying them will turn a person from darkness to light and from death to life.[2] But take care not to imply to anyone that becoming a Christian, infusing the power of the resurrected Christ into his life, will necessarily makes things rosier. Assurance of eternal life, joy at the forgiveness of sin, the power to live a godly life—yes, these are wonderful changes. But to many, choosing such a course means even greater alienation and heartache, more pain and trial. They must rest in the simple truths listed above; all the other things Christians have argued about for centuries will seem as petty as they are.

Majoring on the majors will also mean recognizing the urgency of the moment. The true story is told of a couple who sat one night and planned how to reach a neighbor with the message of the gospel. The neighbor was a young husband and father of two little sons. He appeared successful, with a good job and a decent income. Yet things were not right at home.

The man was a heavy drinker, a sexual addict, and a compulsive spender. He would disappear for days at a time, only to return to the relief of his wife and the delighted squeals of his children.

The couple who had him in their sights had stellar motives. They knew he needed an anchor in the universe, a relationship with God. They decided on a course of social interaction, friendship, reaching out, winning his confidence, earning the right to be heard. The next day, they decided, the wife would talk to the neighbor's wife about getting together.

The Christian woman heard from the neighbor lady much earlier than she had planned, however. At dawn, with her husband already gone to work, she opened the door to the ashen, terrified neighbor who could hardly speak. "He's, he's, he's—" was all she could say, pointing down the street.

When she could communicate, the awful truth came out. Her husband had come home late. They had had an argument. She went to bed alone. Assuming he was asleep downstairs, she slept. When she awoke, she went to check on him and found a note of apology on the kitchen table. Then she found her husband in the garage, dead from self-inflicted carbon monoxide poisoning.

The Christian couple learned a hard lesson. The differences in life-style that had delayed their approach to the neighbor were the very reasons he needed what they had. Their strategy was now moot, their motives irrelevant. All they could say was, "Why do we always wait?" Don't wait to communicate the most important truths—crucial and urgent in their simplicity.

Majoring on the majors also involves not getting hung up on externals. Don't separate yourself from those who disagree with you, inside or outside the faith. It's time to mature, to rise above lists of do's and don'ts—as serviceable as they may have been in your formative years—and begin to see the big picture. When you broaden your worldview and start to see larger issues through the eyes of Christ, you'll find yourself changing in surprising ways.

For instance, if you asked yourself whether the fashions people wear are as important as the intentions of their hearts, you would instinctively know the answer. But do we live that way? Do we respect and admire the ones with the missionary's heart who give of themselves to serve others as much as we do the people comfortable in their wealth and looking as if they posed for the cover of a Yuppie fashion catalogue? Secretly, privately, we probably know which are the people of most depth and character. But whom would we rather socialize with, be seen with, invite over, or be invited over by?

Can you grasp, despite the lie of the TV and movie screen, that some of the most wonderful people you could ever hope to befriend are physically unattractive? Hollywood would have us believe that the leaders, the important, the cool, the stars are handsome, beautiful, articulate, bright. But when we buy into that lie, we find ourselves gravitating toward people who are skin deep. Character has nothing to do with appearances. "The Lord does not see as man sees; for man looks at the outward appearance, but the Lord looks at the heart."[3]

The world worships at the shrine of fashion and culture, but the longer you're in the kingdom, the more you'll see the fallacy of a class system based on such externals. It's been a fascinating discovery to find depth and intelligence, caring and character in people with whom I might not have wanted to be seen when I was in high school.

Where had these people been all my life? Relegated to second-class citizenship by the "in" crowd, assumed to be bookish or nerdy, somehow out of it because they weren't blessed with clear faces, straight teeth, or taut bodies, let alone the money to drape themselves with finery.

The cruelest joke on those who would look down their noses at the less attractive is that in many cases, the years have a way of evening the score. Consider a young woman who turns no heads in high school, yet those who take the time to get to know her find her a woman of humor, compassion, caring, and intelligence. Her opposite—the perky, popular cutie with all the attention—may have little going for her but looks and possessions. What happens when the years bring lines to her face and inches to her waist? Suddenly the two women appear much the same, but the former has behind her a lifetime of joy and service that gives her warm, homely smile a depth of character. The latter becomes hard and bitter over the loss of the externals, those fleeting pretenders that promised more than they ever delivered.

Right now you may not find yourself attracted to or interested in the unlovely. But if you can major on the majors spiritually, you can major on the majors in personal relationships, too. Stand apart from the crowd, and be the one to make the first move across shallow class lines. Include in your orbit those who have more to offer than mere externals. You'll discover treasures of personality and depth, and you'll avoid the shame of lost years by making this find earlier than most.

Not until mature adulthood do we generally realize what's truly important in people. Loyalty. Love. Commitment. Duty. Sacrifice. Diligence. Spirituality. Discipline. Consistency. Don't come to the realization too late that such qualities come in packages of all shapes, sizes, colors, and wrappings. Determine what the majors are now, and major on them for a lifetime. You'll regret the loss if you wait too long.

four. keep short accounts

i hope by now that I'm merely reminding you of truths you learned and saw modeled in our home. (Of course, there are certain things I wish you'd remember and others I'd rather you forgot!) One of them is the importance of keeping short accounts. This practice will fill your life with joy and keep you from painful regrets. I'm not talking here about money; that comes later.

Rather, I'm concerned about interpersonal relationships. What does it mean to keep a short account with a friend or loved one? It means, as Scripture makes clear, to not let anger fester, to not go to bed mad at someone, to "not let the sun go down on your wrath."[1] In other words, get things straight, get them right, before you fall asleep each night.

You know full well that you can hold someone hostage emotionally by withholding forgiveness, refusing to pay back the psychological IOUs of life. What a delicious—and ugly—sense of power that brings. Someone has wronged you, and you both know it. The other person wants to reconcile. You let him squirm for a day, two days, a week. Call me extreme, but I believe that every minute you let that person dangle in a patently anti-Christlike fashion makes you infinitely more guilty than he, regardless of the offense.

The same is true when you're on the other side of the fence, of course. You have wronged someone. You owe a confession, an apology, an "I'm sorry, I was wrong." How freeing, what a relief to see yourself clearly and decide to make the first move! You're disappointed in yourself, sure. You're embarrassed and ashamed. You'd rather not have to admit such weakness. But you do it anyway, and the relationship is wonderfully restored, all the stronger for the pain endured on both sides.

Be assured that I'm aware forgiveness isn't always easily bestowed, and not just because of our addiction to the power that comes from withholding it. Sometimes the hurt is too severe, the pain too deep for a mere oral confrontation and airing of the wrong. I would not heap guilt on you when you find forgiving difficult. In some cases, it may take years and require outside help. My point here, however, is that your role is to communicate, to keep everything on the table, to be sure you're not the one who impedes reconciliation when the time comes.

Yet even in the matter of interpersonal differences, why do I emphasize short accounts? Why not enjoy the manipulative power of having the ball in your court for a few days, exacting a toll of vengeance?

First, of course, is that " 'Vengeance is Mine; I will repay,' says the Lord."[2] If righteous wrath is appropriate, if revenge is to be exacted, that is God's purview. I don't know why. Perhaps it's an admonition for us. Such a reality puts things in perspective. Do we really need or want revenge? Enough to leave it in the hands of God? Sounds severe, doesn't it? Is the offense you're so upset about worth turning over to the One who could exact vengeance with a vengeance? God is saying, in essence, "Vengeance is mine; forgiveness and reconciliation I'll let you handle on your own."

Even when allowed to handle the divine work of forgiving, we should feel a humility born of knowing that God has granted us entrée into His domain. Could you, on your own, forgive someone? Could you, without the power of the Almighty, humble yourself and seek forgiveness from someone else? It's in this doing of godly things that we realize what the apostle Paul meant when he so frequently referred to the power of the resurrected Christ. At one point Paul clarified that "if the Spirit of Him who raised Jesus from the dead dwells in you, He who raised Christ from the dead will also give life to your mortal bodies through His Spirit who dwells in you."[3]

So, I don't say flippantly that this forgiving and being forgiven is human business. It is only because the same Spirit that raised Jesus from the dead dwells in us that we can do those things we wouldn't be able to do by ourselves. We still have the freedom to ignore that power, of course, to wrest control of our own consciences, to allow our old natures to wallow in self-righteousness and what we feel is justified anger and revenge.

Now, another reason for my emphasis on short accounts:

"You do not know what will happen tomorrow. For what is your life? It is even a vapor that appears for a little time and then vanishes away."[4]

Sadly, that New Testament verse cuts both ways. At your age (sorry), you feel invincible. Death is something that happens to someone else. But we never know, do we? True, as we get older we lose more friends, acquaintances, and relatives. But you'll rue the day you put off making things right with someone simply because it seemed there was plenty of time.

A father and son, on their way to a softball game, within sight and sound of their loves ones, inexplicably hit a train and were gone in seconds.

People who knew them said an open Bible was found in the wreckage and that it was not uncommon for them to read to each other in the car. Their accounts with God were likely in good standing. If others of the family had problems with them, they'll live the rest of their lives wishing they had made things right. That wouldn't affect where the men are today, but it would certainly affect the well-being and consciences of the ones they left behind.

A woman, her mother, and her best friend, driving in the country, were struck broadside at a blind intersection. The mother and the best friend were thrown from the car and died within minutes. The woman was injured, and though she would recover, she could not attend the funerals of her mother or her friend. Thankfully, her accounts had been kept short. Arguments, disagreements, and the petty differences of everyday life with a friend and a mother had been dealt with regularly. The deep grief over her devastating losses was not compounded by guilt.

Don't assume the relationship with that former friend will work itself out someday when you're both older.

Pete Maravich, the legendary college and pro basketball star, had often said he hoped he wouldn't play ten years in the National Basketball Association and then die of a heart attack at age 40. That became a sadly accurate prophecy, however. An unknown heart defect felled him as he played in a pickup game a few years after he had retired from a decade in pro ball. He left a wife and young children but thankfully had kept short accounts. He had become a Christian, a dynamic witness and speaker, and had nurtured his family in the faith. Imagine the pain if he and his wife had allowed an argument, some offense, to come between them for a few days, assuming they had plenty of time to work it out and make up.

Instead, Pete Maravich left us with happy, fun stories. He was one of those joyously gifted players born to pass, shoot, and score. He passed behind his back, between opponents' legs, and over his shoulder without looking. He once opened an Atlanta Hawks game against the Houston Rockets by bringing the ball up the floor to just across mid-court and firing a no-look, behind-the-back pass all the way to a teammate in the corner. The teammate shot before the Rockets knew the ball had been passed, and the Hawks never trailed in the game.

Legends also abound of Pistol Pete, as he was known, burning to share his faith. He would take to the streets, find kids in neighborhood basketball games, and ask if he could talk to them about something important. They were always wary. He was not unusually tall, so without his uniform and his trademark floppy socks, they often didn't recognize him. The kids would turn him down. Maybe they suspected a sermon. He would ask if he could play. They would turn him down again.

Then he would challenge them. "How about me against all of you, and if I win, I get to talk to you for a few minutes?"

That challenge was almost always accepted. Pete played against as many as six players at once, dashing about the asphalt, batting shots away, stealing the ball, dribbling around and through everyone for lay-ups and getting free for long outside shots. Soon his style of play gave away his identity and the kids wanted autographs. But first he made them live up to their part of the bargain. No one knows how many kids were led to Christ by Pete Maravich's unusual approach. But some are eternally grateful he didn't put off till tomorrow something he did that day.

It would have been easy for Pete to say, "Hey, the average man lives to about 70. There's plenty of time for serving the Lord." Pete himself had grown up in an abusive, dysfunctional home and had become an alcoholic. In his mind, he had already wasted too many years. As soon as he could, he began serving the Lord. Only a few years later, he was gone.

In making a point with His disciples about covetousness and materialism, Jesus also drove home this point about short accounts. He told them, "Take heed and beware of covetousness, for one's life does not consist in the abundance of the things he possesses." Then He spoke a parable to them, saying: "The ground of a certain rich man yielded plentifully. And he thought within himself, saying, 'What shall I do, since I have no room to store my crops?' So he said, 'I will do this: I will pull down my barns and build greater, and there I will store all my crops and my goods. And I will say to my soul, "Soul, you have many goods laid up for many years; take your ease; eat, drink, and be merry."' But God said to him, 'You fool! This night your soul will be required of you; then whose will those things be which you have provided?' So is he who lays up treasure for himself, and is not rich toward God."[5]

Jesus' point was about misplaced priorities, but notice His emphasis also on the fact that "*this night* your soul will be required of you" (italics added).

Since before you were born, this world has seen prominent people cut down in the prime of their lives. Presidential assassinations are always historic, of course, but it seems the 1963 shooting of John Kennedy launched decades of mayhem that saw Martin Luther King, Jr., Bobby Kennedy, John Lennon, Anwar Sadat, and many others shot to death. Fired upon have been Gerald Ford, Ronald Reagan, and the Pope. Killed in plane crashes have been noted pop stars like Buddy Holly and Ricky Nelson, as well as Christian singer and songwriter Keith Green. The list goes on and on.

The sad, macabre fact is that we can't know from one moment to the next what might happen. With the recent renewed interest in the Kennedy slayings have come replay after replay of the moments leading up to the deaths of both the president and his brother. I'm always struck by the warmth of the smiles just before the tragedies. Think about it. Seconds before being shot to death, John Kennedy was waving and smiling. His lovely, young wife was basking in the adoration of the parade crowd.

Five years later, Bobby had just won the California Democratic presidential primary and appeared headed for nomination and maybe the White House. He and his aides were ecstatic and had just received congratulations from frenzied followers before turning away from the podium. Less than a minute later, he lay mortally wounded.

We don't know the details of the lives of these fate-crossed luminaries. History shows there was pain and strain in their personal lives. They were not and could not have been as happy and carefree as their smiles indicated. But certainly they did not expect to die in the next second. Surely they had planned to deal with personal issues.

But no matter how short their accounts, they weren't short enough.

If the fear of imminent death—yours or your friend's—is too remote to motivate you to regularly mend relationships, then do it for peace of mind. Living with a muddied conscience can be a fate worse than death anyway. I covet for you short accounts, loving, giving, selfless relationships, and an ability to apologize unequivocally when necessary.

five. learn to apologize unconditionally

his may seem to you too narrow a subject for its own chapter. Perhaps it seems merely an element of the previous topic. But trust me, this is an area crucial enough to deserve its own space.

Recent years have seen a deluge of material published on interpersonal relationships and a push to make people aware of the need to verbalize their feelings. Yet this matter of full-blown apologizing has been neglected.

Many people know they should apologize when they're wrong, and sometimes they do. But those apologies often serve as little more than excuses to get in the last word. "Well, I'm sorry, but if you hadn't . . ." That's a typical nonapologetic apology.

Another unacceptable excuse for an apology is illustrated by the story of a pastor who had unintentionally offended an elderly parishioner named Margaret. He had remarked in public about the wisdom and understanding that had come with her many years, yea, decades of devotion to Christ.

Clearly he was trying to compliment Margaret, but she turned stone cold and walked away. She even stayed out of church. She didn't follow the biblical mandate about an offense. ("Moreover if your brother sins against you, go and tell him his fault between you and him alone. If he hears you, you have gained your brother."[1])

Rather, she complained to others, and the word got back to the pastor. Now, plainly, Margaret was wrong. She had misunderstood, taken offense at something intended as a compliment, and then compounded the problem by spreading discord. Though she had intentionally bad-mouthed the unsuspecting pastor, she would not set foot inside the church again until he apologized for innocently insulting her.

Despite her total misunderstanding and inappropriate reaction, here was a chance for the pastor to rectify the situation with an unequivocal, unconditional, nonargumentative, nonalibic (I apologize for making up that word) apology. The right thing to do here, even in his innocence, was to immediately go to her. He should have said, "Margaret, I was wrong. What I said was insensitive, and I'm sorry. I want you to forgive me, because I love you and regret saying anything that would indicate otherwise."

How would she have reacted? She might have realized she had been mistaken. How could a man who cared this much have meant to offend her? She then would have accepted the apology, offered forgiveness, and probably admitted she had been thin-skinned. She also might have passed off the offense as a generational misunderstanding.

Margaret might even have felt guilty about spreading the bad word about the pastor and asked his forgiveness for that. She knew she had not confronted him, but here he was apologizing. Of course, when people complain to friends about the conduct of others, they are either very careful to whom they talk, or they secretly hope the word will get back, which was the case here.

But let me tell you what actually happened. The pastor took offense at Margaret's offense. He found it ludicrous that she could possibly react as she did, so he defended himself. To anyone who had heard the story, he pleaded his case, garnering as much support as he could. Though she had been a beloved saint in the church since long before he had come, he believed others would agree she was wrong. And many did. When he recounted his version of the conversation, most agreed she had misunderstood and was out of line. However, for the sake of unity and in the spirit of Christ, their counsel was that he make the first move. "Go to her," they said, "and apologize."

"For what?" he replied indignantly. "Not only did I not insult her, but I was even trying to compliment her! What should I be sorry for?"

"For the fact that you offended her."

For a couple of weeks he refused. He was right. She was wrong. It was her place to come to him. If she didn't want to come to church, what could he do about it? He wasn't going to beg.

When the third Sunday rolled around and still Margaret was nowhere to be seen (word had it she wasn't attending anywhere else, either, but was home wallowing in self-pity), she became the prime topic of conversation in the congregation. Factions arose. She was always a troublemaker at heart, some said. The pastor is being stubborn, said others. He must do the right thing because it's the right thing, regardless of who's in the wrong.

The pressure became so intense that the pastor was forced to seek out Margaret. But he had waited so long that she was angry and wouldn't allow him in her house. She opened the door, glared at him, and demanded, "What do you want?"

"I want to know what's bothering you. We've missed you at church, and I understand I've offended you."

"You have."

Now get this. His response was pivotal. It allowed him to say later that he had made the first move, that he had apologized, and that she had not accepted it. In fact, however, what he said made her shut the door in his face. "I'm sorry you feel that way," he replied, "because that certainly wasn't what I meant."

Do you hear what she heard? That was no apology but an accusation. He may not have meant to do that, either, but what he told her, in essence, was, "You were wrong. You misunderstood. Your offense is frivolous. What I'm sorry about is that you feel as you do and are mistaken."

The poor woman didn't return to her lifelong church until three years later, when that pastor moved on. Make no mistake, she was wrong. She had misunderstood the pastor's words and then reacted improperly. But he exacerbated the situation by his refusal to offer an unconditional apology.

Am I suggesting you should lie by apologizing when you're not sorry? No. Rather, I'm saying that if you have offended someone, you *should be* sorry, even if the other person misunderstood. Taking responsibility for someone else's lack of understanding is no sacrifice. Make the apology. Restore the relationship. Later, when you're both more rational, the day may come when you can explain yourself.

People of our generation, and especially older folks, have little experience in apologizing overtly. For some reason, it must have appeared weak in the past. If someone was sorry about an outburst or an action, he or she might try to make up for it by obviously doing something for the offended individual or being unusually nice and deferential. The parent who screamed in rage over some small infraction would realize the mistake and change for a while. That was intended as an apology. But kids, depending on their age and experience, often didn't catch it. They were glad Mom or Dad was back on keel and not so frightening, but the account had never been settled. There had never been closure. An inappropriate reaction had occurred and was never explained, apologized for, or forgiven.

Where I failed on that score with you, I apologize. I am truly sorry, and I want always to be able to look you in the eye and say so.

I learned much from a man who once shamed himself in front of his daughter. He was on his way to drop her off at preschool when another driver cut him off and honked. The man, a Christian who didn't swear, cheat, or steal, suddenly found himself making an obscene gesture to the other driver! He prayed his daughter had not noticed, but she had.

"Daddy," she said, "did you just stick up your swear finger at that man?"

"Naw," he said. "I was just waving. I thought I knew him."

He says she accepted his explanation and appeared to forget the incident. But of course he didn't. Until it was time to pick her up, his lie tormented him. To have done the thing in the first place was horrifying to him, but to compound it with a lie to his own daughter!

Remember, this girl was a preschooler, four years old. What was he to do? He considered confessing, telling her the truth, disappointing her with the reality that he had done something out of character and unacceptable, something that might cloud her view of him. He didn't want to equivocate if he did apologize, either, trying to explain that he had done it instinctively, in anger.

By the time he returned to pick her up, he knew he had no choice. His conscience would not allow the lie to stand between them. When she got in the car, he asked her to look him in the eye and listen carefully, because there was something very important he needed to say. He says it was the toughest thing he's ever done, including telling his boss he was quitting a job after the boss had gone to bat for him with the brass.

"When you asked me this morning if I had stuck up my swear finger at that man," he said, "I told you no. But I was lying. I didn't want you to think I would do something like that, but I did. I'm sorry I did it, and I'm even more sorry I lied to you about it. I asked God to forgive me, and I want you to forgive me, too."

Her eyes widened as he told her, but he couldn't read whether she was shocked, disappointed, or impressed. She reached up and hugged him. "Of course I forgive you, Daddy," she said happily. It was as if he had been forgiven anew by God Himself.

My friend believes that experience set him on a course of being quick to apologize to his children. When he overreacts, he apologizes; when he's been short or irritable, he says he's sorry. If he breaks a promise, he admits it and makes it right. When he's wrong in an argument, he comes clean. He believes his kids appreciate that and are quicker to take responsibility for their own actions because of his example.

Interestingly, he recently asked his daughter, now a teenager, if she remembered the preschool incident. To his amazement, she did not. She now found it amusing, and he wished he hadn't recounted it. Apparently the apology had made the offense much less traumatic to her than to him, and he would have done better to have left it alone now.

Apologies thwart our natural tendencies toward self-righteousness. We don't want to become namby-pamby milquetoasts, running around saying we're sorry for everything that goes wrong, as if everything is our fault. But when we've failed or offended, we should have enough practice to apologize naturally. Fully. Completely. Unequivocally.

Almost as important as being able to apologize is being able to accept an apology. When we're forgiving someone is not the time to lecture. "You ought to be sorry" is clearly not the proper response. You should know from experience that apologies are difficult enough. They should be accepted at face value, and forgiveness should be granted. The thing to say is not, "Well, I forgive you, but . . ." Rather, it is simply, "I accept your apology, and I forgive you."

Take care not to denigrate people or their apologies by saying, "Oh, that's all right. Forget it." If they feel a matter is important enough to apologize for, they did something wrong—at least in their own eyes. That should be honored with an appropriate response.

Someone has said that the toughest five words in the English language—and the rarest—are "I'm sorry. I was wrong." May that never be so with you.

PART THREE

between you and God

six. nourish the inner life

he following message may be tougher to give than to receive. For what confidence must one have to exhort another to remain consistent in his spiritual life? Lest there be some illusion that I've mastered the life of devotion, let me dispel it right now. However, rather than lapsing into do-as-I-say-and-not-as-I-do, let me try a few things on you that have worked for me over the years.

First, resist the temptation to turn over a new leaf and establish a rigorous, daily schedule that will satisfy you only if you keep it meticulously. Unless you're one in a thousand, you will set yourself up for disappointment and failure, not for losing your zeal for Christ, but rather for not living up to your own unrealistic goals.

In other words, don't vow that you'll spend an hour every morning at six studying the Bible, reading a commentary, enjoying a devotional book, reading a Christian self-help tome, and covering your entire prayer list. Those would be worthy goals, of course, and there may be one day each week when you would do well to wrestle such an hour into position as your top priority.

But what happens when you've stayed out late, are studying for an exam, are ill, or are simply lazy? Will the practice and the vow go out the window, along with your self-esteem? As one who tends to be a perfectionist and enjoys planning with lofty goals, let me suggest something more realistic.

Any time you decide that studying your way through a good Christian book will benefit you and draw you closer to Christ, do it. No one said you had to read a chapter a day and never miss a day for two weeks. Put the book where you have easy access to it, and when you want to and can, dip into it. Take a note or two. Pray over it. Have your Bible handy. Look at verses in context. If you don't get back to the book for a few days, don't beat yourself up over it.

When you finish, talk about it. Tell a friend what you learned.

Recommend the book. Friends will begin to reciprocate, and you can try books they've enjoyed and learn more about them (the books *and* the friends) in the process. That can draw you closer to Christian brothers and sisters, another benefit.

Best of all, such reading, studying, and discussing can give you practical help in your Christian life. Do you ever feel frustrated, knowing you need guidance yet wondering how you'll recognize it when God sends it? His Word is the best place to start, of course, and then exposing yourself to the thinking of other students of the Book can only help you focus better.

For example, many Christians, young and old, are frustrated by their inability to put into practice the promise of the verse that tells us God will provide a way of escape from any temptation.[1] Too often they don't realize that the basics, daily Bible reading and prayer, will give them the ammunition they need.

Prayer is something that need not be relegated to devotional times. You know of people who "think" prayers, "breathe" prayers, and, as Scripture encourages, "pray without ceasing."[2] No matter where you are or what you're doing, you can be in contact, in communion, communicating with God. He can help you as you witness, study, take a test, face a temptation, work out—even eat. That constant contact, in my opinion, is a key to the life of faith and is more important than a daily regimen or ritual, helpful as that might be.

I certainly don't want to denigrate regular, daily devotions. Some of the most dynamic and vibrant Christians I know have found such discipline critical to their spiritual survival. Scripture is replete with admonitions to daily seek God through His Word. The psalmist said he will sing praise to God's name forever, so that he can daily perform what he has promised.[3]

When you consider that God is regular and consistent with His blessing and work in our lives,[4] it should make you want to reciprocate. We're not divine, and we can't approximate God, but we can show our devotion. Whether it be in a formal, set-aside time with aids and manuals or simply with our thoughts and prayers, "daily He shall be praised."[5]

God calls righteous those who seek Him daily and delight to know His ways. "They take delight in approaching God."[6]

As the apostle Paul wrote to the Corinthians, the most important thing we Christians can do daily is die[7]—die to ego, to self, to our fleshly desires. We must decrease so He might increase.[8] That's easier said than done, of course. What does it mean to die daily, and why can't we do it once and for all? You know, some can and do; I know a few of them.

If you've ever tried to die to yourself—to put your wishes and desires in the background and serve Christ, others, or the church—you know that soon the flesh feels deprived. It's as if your whole being cries out, "Hey, how about something for Number One?"

I've read that Billy Graham set his pride and ego aside at an early point in his ministry and told the Lord, in essence, "I know who I am and who I am not." Basically, he got out of the way so God could use him.

On the other hand, Luis Palau, another international evangelist, admits that he has to die daily. He says his pride and ego fight for preeminence, and he has to constantly remind himself and be reminded by the Holy Spirit to pray for humility and selflessness.

While I greatly admire Dr. Graham and see him as perhaps the leading believer of this century, I have to say I can identify more easily with Dr. Palau. My guess is that you, too, will find his pattern more common in your life. Decreasing so Christ can increase means sublimating your own desires and pleasures for the sake of His will. That doesn't mean He doesn't want you to enjoy life. But the more your self-centered will comes to the fore, the less Christ will be manifested in your life.

Now let me shift gears and appear to go against all the precautionary advice here so far. Two aspects of the life of devotion to Christ must be prioritized and committed to: regular church attendance and daily Scripture reading. These are primary to the survival of the spiritual life and are, sadly, the first things to go by the wayside—at least temporarily—when someone gets out on his or her own.

Whether this happens due to laziness or simply a testing of one's own wings, who can say? There's a great headiness in finally being "out from under" and able to make your own decisions, set your own schedule, suffer for your own mistakes, and benefit from your own initiative.

Too many people exercise their new freedom by relaxing their spiritual disciplines, dropping out of church for months, and becoming lax in their Bible reading. You will want to explore, to try new things, to expose yourself to a variety of worship styles. But do yourself a favor and make a pact, not with me or with God, but with yourself. Decide in advance that no matter how much church shopping you do, or what different things you try in the exercise of your faith, you will not put that spiritual life on hold even for a season.

Just as the body loses its tone when exercise lapses, the spiritual life atrophies when starved of the basics that help it grow. For some reason, there is no such thing as stagnation in the Christian life. You're either growing or dying. You can't stand still.

Yes, there will be times when your job or your schoolwork makes your normal Sunday morning routine impossible. That might be the day to stay home and do what you have to do: recuperate from a hellacious week of exams, catch up on a pressing project, or fulfill an obligation you absolutely could not get to otherwise. But at the end of the day, when you've changed your routine to meet your legitimate purposes, why not catch an evening service somewhere? Try a new church. Go with a friend. Or even go to a church where you know no one.

If you absolutely must take a Sunday off from church to maintain your sanity or your health, do it occasionally. What you want to avoid is dropping out for weeks and months at a time. You may have every intention of "getting back into it," but you will find yourself more and more distracted, more enamored of your extra time, more and more pleased with your independence. Even if and when the day comes that you find you've missed what the Bible calls "the assembling of ourselves together,"[9] you will sadly discover that you can never replace the lost time.

Interestingly, in that passage where the writer to the Hebrews exhorted them to "forsake not" the assembling, he added, "as is the manner of some." Rather, he continued, "exhort[ing] one another." Now there's an archaic concept if you've ever heard one! When was the last time you were exhorted by someone outside your family? In this day and age, we live for ourselves, make our own decisions, are self-sufficient. To exhort someone else is to risk being told off and shunned. Yet there it is in Scripture.

Maybe overt exhortation has gone out of style. But showing up in church regularly will be a silent exhortation to others that they should do the same. And seeing others there week after week for Bible study and worship will show you that it can be done, should be done, that other people see the value and dire need for the assembling.

We all know there are phonies and hypocrites in the church. That's the oldest and weakest argument for staying away. We should go because of those very weaknesses recognized in ourselves. We go so that we can grow out of phoniness and into genuine faith practice. We want to be less hypocritical and more devout. We go because we're needy, not because we have something to offer.

Now the matter of daily Bible reading. This is an embarrassingly sticky point for most believers, because so few are successful at maintaining it. Few Christians have read through the Bible, and fewer still can stay with a regular program. Let me suggest something that has worked for me.

After a lifetime of inconsistency and frustration in this area, I realized I was most comfortable in letting others interpret Scripture for me. I had been quite a Bible memory whiz as a child, and most of those verses stayed with me. Occasionally I would think them through and try to figure out what they meant, sometimes even peeking into a commentary for help. But daily Bible reading? Always a failure. Trying to read through the whole thing? February and Exodus usually did me in.

One year I got serious. I bought myself one of those one-year Bibles, where the passages have not only been suggested but have also been placed chronologically in the book. Your Old and New Testament readings, your Psalms, and your Proverbs are all laid out for you right in a row. All you have to do is read between ten and twenty minutes a day, every day for a year, and you will have read through the whole Bible.

Let me make a confession. I chose the easiest translation I could find, because once and for all—despite a lifetime in church and Sunday school—I wanted to get the whole picture and have some idea what I was reading.

I happened to find the early morning impossible because my daily reading was then determined by how early I arose as compared to when my first appointment was. Reading at lunchtime was hit and miss, too. If I missed a day or two, I could easily make it up, but the best and most efficient way to make this a habit, I knew, was to do it at the same time every day for weeks.

I finally hit upon the one time in the day that was predictable—bedtime. I knew that no matter where I was in the world or what else was happening in my life, at some point late in the evening or in the wee hours of the morning, I was going to fall asleep somewhere. I committed to making my daily Bible reading, with that through-the-Bible-in-a-year tool, the last thing I did every night before going to sleep.

I know there are all kinds of reasons why maybe that wasn't the best idea. Often I was so tired that I rushed, not catching everything. After reading, I wasn't praying, I was sleeping. I wasn't thinking, either, at least consciously. But the fact is, I was getting my Bible reading in.

I wish I could express to you the benefits. I got a picture of the whole scope of Scripture. I got a sense of the flow of history, of how the whole thing, Old and New Testaments, fit together. I enjoyed a daily sense of accomplishment. All I had to do was a little planning ahead. If I was on the road, I took the book with me. At home, I left it at my bedside. When I occasionally fell a few days behind, rather than trying to catch up all at once, I just read two daily portions a day for several days and was right back on track.

At the end of that first year, I had for the first time fulfilled a New Year's resolution. Admittedly, I had done it as an obligation at first. And yes, there were days when I wished I hadn't made the commitment. But I wouldn't trade the experience for anything, and I have done it several times since. I look forward to it. It's the best habit I can recommend.

Well, that was a long-winded way to say, "Read your Bible and go to church," but that's what it all boils down to. I promise not to check up on you. You're on your own now, and you make your own decisions. But I pray you'll always consider the care and feeding of your spiritual life your top priority.

seven. remain sexually pure

nyone in church and in the Word knows that Scripture is clear about sex. It's beautiful, it's fun, it was God's idea, it's required for procreation, and it's restricted to the marriage bed.

Why? The question rings from those who for years have accused God of being a cosmic killjoy. Why couldn't He have left adultery out of the Ten Commandments? Why did He invent something that exciting, fun, and satisfying and not let us enjoy it with anyone of our choice?

At the risk of offending those looking over our shoulders here, those who think it's always wrong to include the Bible in a joke (to a point, I agree), let me describe a cartoon I once saw. It depicted Moses returning from Mount Sinai to the Israelites. He was saying, to the best of my recollection, "The good news is I've got Him down from 17 commandments to ten. The bad news is, adultery is still in."

Yes, Scripture is clear. Engaging in sexual activity with someone other than your spouse is sin. It's wrong. It's off limits. And it has consequences. But is it wrong merely because God says so, or does He say so because He knows something we don't?

The secular entertainment and publishing businesses have been attacking, for the last 25 years or so, the old-fashioned views of sexuality. Our bodies are beautiful, they say. Love is uplifting and rewarding. Sex between consenting adults should be encouraged, rewarded, recommended.

People we might otherwise admire and respect because they're "nice guys" or they're articulate, bright, or talented sleep around, live with unmarried partners, and have children out of wedlock.

This flies in the face of Scripture, which says, "For this is the will of God, your sanctification: that you should abstain from sexual immorality. . . . For God did not call us to uncleanness, but in holiness."[1] But they get away with it. They are exalted, famous, wealthy, beautiful, popular. Is it really so wrong?

Theologians, scholars, pastors, and others who know the Word much more thoroughly than I could ever hope to tell me that for every prohibition God gives in Scripture, He also presents at least two rewards for abstaining. He doesn't always tell His reasons, but He has them nonetheless.

One reason we can be so sure about what God desires in this area is that His counsel comes couched with the phrase "the will of God." As you know, some people spend much of their lives agonizing over how to determine God's will. They put out fleeces, seek counsel, pray for hours, make lists of pros and cons, and try to ferret out the answer to the mystery. Yet on this score, Scripture says, flat out, "This is the will of God."

The apostle Paul told the Romans that they should not be conformed to this world, "but be transformed by the renewing of your mind, that you may prove what is that good and acceptable and perfect will of God."[2] In other words, no matter how attractive or beguiling is the person who would sell you on open sexuality, he or she is part of this world. Renew your mind, get it out of the world's logic, the world's system, and you will be transformed. Why? So you can prove what is the will of God.

Thus, we're back to the will of God. The apostle Peter, who had a lot to say on the subject, wrote, "For this is the will of God, that by doing good you may put to silence the ignorance of foolish men."[3] We don't even have to pray about that one. When the Bible says, "For this is the will of God," that's a fairly straightforward clue. And that will is? That our doing good puts to silence the ignorance of foolish people, even those ridiculously attractive and idolized stars who flaunt their freedom to do what they want sexually.

That first verse I quoted in this chapter made clear that the will of God is "your sanctification," which was defined as abstaining from sexual immorality.

Forgive me for being didactic here, but you know I'm no scholar. Such things come to me in bits and pieces, fragments from here and there. You're probably already way ahead of me, but except for the big why question, we have established that the will of God can be known. And the will of God for us is that we be sanctified and abstain from sexual immorality. Of course, the will of God is much broader than that, and at other places in the Bible, that telltale phrase clues us in that what's coming next is worth knowing. (A good personal study sometime.)

If we believe the Bible, the world is wrong and God is right on this. To us, in our flesh, that may not sound so good. Does the world have a better, more fun idea? Why is our heavenly Father such a stickler on this? Logic tells us He has His reasons. What are they?

"The world is passing away, and the lust of it; but he who does the will of God abides forever."⁴ That verse indicates we have a choice. We can say God is a not a fun guy and then satisfy our lust to our peril. Or we can do God's will—which includes abstaining from sexual impurity—and live forever.

When I'm pondering God's reasons for such prohibitions as this one, the answer occasionally comes from the world. Isn't that interesting? The Bible says that sometimes God will use "the foolish things of the world to put to shame the wise," and "the weak things of the world to put to shame the things which are mighty."⁵ I always took that to mean—and I'm sure it does—that He uses things and people (like us) who appear foolish to confound people who are considered wise. But sometimes, maybe just for fun, He uses the "ignorance of [the world's] foolish men" to teach us Christians something.

I read in a newspaper advice column about a girl who had lost her virginity at a party. She and her boyfriend got drunk, and she ignored her inhibitions. They had sex for the first time. He lost respect for and interest in her, and she also wound up pregnant. Telling her parents was an ordeal, and resisting their efforts to have her abort the child took all her resolve. She told the advice columnist that she was trying to make up for what she had done wrong by doing one thing right: keeping the child and raising it herself.

She did that and was glad she did, but her story was a sad litany of remorse and heartache. She felt rejected, like damaged goods. She felt she had been robbed of her childhood, of what might have been her most fun years. Nobody wanted to marry a young girl with a child. Her parents tried to help, but she still had to work full-time.

Here is a girl—a child, really—forced to take adult responsibility for the next 20 years because of a mistake. The advice columnist, known for a generally liberal bias (including recommending that engaged couples live together for a while), made the wry statement that maybe there was something after all to this quaint idea of remaining a virgin until marriage. What a novel idea!

Skeptics will say the problem there was drunkenness, not sex. But what about those couples who take every precaution (they get enough public help for that) and still find themselves pregnant? Then they feel they must resort to the ultimate form of birth control, abortion.

Innocence is lost. Respect is lost. Love is often lost. Lifetimes of guilt and remorse result. Even with the new, so-called enlightened views of sexuality, there's still a stigma attached to children with no last name and to women—it's always the women who bear the brunt—who "couldn't control themselves." Men, because of the ancient double standard and the fact that their pregnancies are borne by someone else and thus don't show, seemingly escape more easily the sins of their youth.

The fact is that for both offending parties, life will never be the same as it was. Virginity and purity are not restorable qualities. Short of the forgiveness of God and conversion to Christ, there is no starting over, no going back and making things right.

Sexually transmitted diseases (STDs) have been around for a very long time. But now, with deadly AIDS on the rampage, we're long past the time when getting an STD meant just a few days of discomfort relieved by doses of penicillin. Some say this is the judgment of God. Regardless, such dangers are clearly the consequences of sin.

If sexual sin can be quantified, adultery can be even worse than premarital fornication. Think of all the lives affected by marital cheating: two marriages, four spouses, their children, extended families, and even friends and acquaintances.

What chaos results in the lives of children! Offending spouses say that kids are resilient, that they handle such things with more maturity than we give them credit for. But ask the kids, even 20 years later, and they'll tell you that the breakup of their parents' marriage was the single most traumatic experience of their lives, the thing they would most like to change.

Whatever insecurities and dysfunction they take into adulthood, they trace them back to the infidelity of one or both of their parents. Even couples who stay together in spite of adultery see their children suffer from the knowledge of the broken trust between their parents.

Think of the precious gift you have to offer the love of your life. A pure body. Your virginity. Something to look forward to on your wedding night. A lifetime of learning and enjoying each other physically. The choice to remain the exclusive property of your spouse for as long as you both live.

Sure, you have other options. Sure, someone somewhere might appear more attractive or alluring or easier to "connect" with. But you will have made a choice, a commitment, a vow. That eliminates your options. But that is no handicap, no sacrifice. Rather, it's something to celebrate. As you age, you may miss the younger version of your partner, but how much sweeter and more fulfilling to cherish the years of devotion and exclusivity!

Trust me, it is an indescribable joy to know you have been sexually faithful to one person for a lifetime of marriage. To be able to live every day with a clean conscience, even about your previous loves and relationships, is a treasure beyond words.

Maintain your guard even when you become engaged so that regardless of the eventualities, you will have honored your love's future spouse. You see what I'm saying? Your intended's future spouse just might not be you. And even if it is, you'll find yourself with a pure relationship when you begin your married life. And if your engagement should end for any reason, sexual impurity will not be one of your regrets.

God's prohibition against sexual immorality is more than a rule that inhibits our pleasure. It is, instead, a framework from which a life of fun, excitement, purity, and commitment can stem. Embrace sexual purity. Plan for it. Guard yourself against failure with a personal list of hedges that protect you against weaknesses and tempting situations.

What might some of those hedges be? Again, it depends on you and your weaknesses. At the risk of being overly frank, are there embraces, kisses, and caresses that make it difficult for you to put the brakes on your sexual passion? Are there places you should not go, planning you should do to keep yourself from situations that would be too tempting?

You know by now that sexual activity is progressive. If your wish is to express your love and devotion, there are ways to do it and ways not to do it. You know yourself, but you also need to know your partner. What activities communicate more than affection? What things begin a progression that will lead only to either sex or frustration? That's where you want to plant your hedges.

When you're married, wouldn't you love to be the first person your spouse ever kissed in a deeply passionate and prolonged way? Wouldn't you love to discover between yourselves all the fun and exciting physical possibilities for lifetime partners, without worrying or wondering whether either of you has already been down those roads? That's the peace of mind you want to extend to the eventual spouse of your current heartthrob— even if that spouse turns out to be you.

Then there's the matter of what you can do with the sexual tension that builds because of your decision to remain pure. Experts say sexual energy can be directed into other pursuits and can even be a power source for sports and studying. To be honest, I always found that energy distracting and wasn't sure how to redirect it. My layman's counsel is that if you can channel sexual energy into some other pursuit, do it and let me know how it turns out. If you're merely distracted trying that, the best and only advice that has ever worked for me is found in the New Testament, where the apostle Paul told young Timothy to flee lust.[6]

Some may say that fleeing lust by doing something else is redirecting sexual energy. Regardless, sometimes it's the only way to remain pure.

Avert your eyes. Avoid that movie. Trash that magazine. Run from that situation. We're not to stand and fight or even pray for strength in the face of sexual temptation. Turn tail and run.

The rewards will be infinitely more satisfying than any moment of sinful pleasure, especially one that could cloud the rest of your life.

PART FOUR

the practical
fundamentals

eight. avoid credit; invest, invest, invest

Y ou know enough to not expect a complex financial lesson from me, despite that chapter title. I'm a black-and-white financial guy, and there are enough Christian experts on the scene if you're interested in seriously investigating the subject. But I can tell you this: Even if you never learn the intricacies of the stock market or what inflation and recession are all about, certain basics can put you in good stead for a lifetime.

While it's true that the love of money is the root of all kinds of evil, "for which some have strayed from the faith in their greediness, and pierced themselves through with many sorrows,"[1] be careful not to be prejudiced against money itself. Too many misread that verse to say that money is the root of evil. Money is not the culprit; the love of money is. Money can, in fact, be managed for great benefit—not just for you and your loved ones, but also for the church.

One of the most common disasters among newly independent young adults is discovering how easily they can have all they want when they want it. The ticket? Credit debt. Just about anyone with an income can get a wallet full of credit cards. Department stores offer their own cards with payment plans so deceptively easy that you can have thousands of dollars worth of merchandise for monthly payments that fit into your budget.

The problem, of course, is that before you know it, your income is committed to numerous easy payment plans that in total are not so easy to manage. And if each purchase is carefully computed, you'll find you're paying much more than the retail price. If you pay the minimum amount each month, you could spend two or three times the original price and consume years paying off each bill.

Did you know that four of five Americans owe more than they own?[2] That all starts somewhere, and for most it begins when they strike out on their own. Who can resist the ease of credit? We want what we want, and we tell ourselves lies: "I'll pay it off early." "I'll pay the whole bill when it arrives."

"I won't buy anything else on credit."

But then some other fantastic deal comes along, something we become convinced we need, though we hadn't thought about it the day before (thank you, Madison Avenue). We get a raise and believe we can work one more small payment into our budgets. Sadly, even if we can afford the payments, buying on credit anything that depreciates is bad business.

I've seen young people talked into high-priced vacuum cleaners, encyclopedia sets (with fashionable, wood-veneer bookcase), cemetery plots, dish sets, knives, pots and pans—you name it. Before they know it, they can barely make their payments. They want a nice car, a vacation, and all the other things their parents worked years for—or, in the worst scenario, went into debt for and thus provided a poor example.

Every raise, every bonus, every surprise check that could have been enjoyed, invested, or given away merely keeps their heads above water. What a depressing way to live! Such a quagmire quickly sucks in even those with the best intentions.

John and Sandy (not their real names) are a couple I know well. They married young and went without some of the nicer things in life because they had little income and no credit. What bank cards they could get had small lines of credit. They were glad to have those when the occasional emergency overtook them, but they found it increasingly difficult to pay the bills. Soon their few cards were maxed out; they were making the minimum payment every month and incurring high interest on the balance.

When both were working, they were finally able to pay off the cards. That would have been the time to start over on a cash basis and plan for those days when Sandy would be home raising children for a few years. But with their combined income, they fell prey to loan companies who extended them larger lines of credit. Here was the chance to have all the stuff their parents had, the things John and Sandy had had to do without when they were first married.

They couldn't resist. They started with just a few of what they considered necessities. Panic set in when their balances began to rise again, but they kept paying and kept signing for new cards. Soon they were in so deep that Sandy had to keep working, right up until the time their first baby was born. And she had to go back to work as soon as she was able, which went against everything they believed and had hoped for. They weren't against a wife's working, but they had hoped she could stay home at least until their children were in school.

Illnesses and crises fell on them the way they do on most couples. There were car problems, sick kids, home repairs—you name it. When

Sandy had to quit her job and they found themselves living on one income, they were barely able to make their payments. It took them more than ten years to dig out and get on a solid financial footing, and both rue the lost years. "It seemed like a black hole," John says. "There was little fun in our lives. We were always behind, always scrambling, dreading the emergency that would put us under."

The answer for you? Budgeting. Firm priorities. And rock-solid principles. For example, credit purchases of depreciable items (virtually everything but a home) must be paid off when the bill comes. Credit cards should be reserved for emergencies, and should such an unanticipated expense set you back, you sacrifice for as long as it takes to retire the debt. Always, always, always earmark some money for saving or investing. If you're skittish or know no one you trust, even putting money in modest interest-bearing accounts is better that frittering it away. A dollar spent unnecessarily today costs several dollars that could have been available to you in the future. But a dollar saved or invested today results in several dollars accessible to you later.

I don't buy into the idea that you can force God to bless you by giving to Him. However, I do believe you cannot out-give God. We're called to be good stewards of all our possessions, not just our money. If you honor God with what you have, He will honor that. It's not a matter of investing in your future by giving to God. The point is showing your devotion to Him by supporting His work, His church, His kingdom. That may or may not make you rich, but if it does, that only gives you more of an opportunity to do more for Him. Avoiding credit debt and investing a certain, budgeted amount regularly will allow you financial freedom. Even if it seems modest, it adds up; and the younger you are when you begin, the greater the accumulation. That allows you to use more and more of your money for God.

I once heard a police officer say that the most dangerous drug anywhere is not LSD or PCPs—it's SFN: something for nothing. The lure of the easy score is the basis for crime, tragedy, disappointment, and ruin. Nearly everyone has a story of the big scam, the can't-miss opportunity, the chance to cash in on an opportunity too good to be true. You've heard the old adage: If it sounds too good to be true, it probably is.

Never believe it when someone (especially in a commercial) tells you this is your last chance to buy an item for this low, low price. Never another sale? The same item won't be offered ever again at a discount? If you see something at a good price, something you've been looking for and have decided you need, make the careful decision. But if you're tempted to make a purchase simply because of a great deal, delay your decision for several days or a week. If the deal is gone, it'll come back around. If it's still available and you're still convinced of your need, you can make the purchase. But if you can't do it with your discretionary cash, you can't afford it. That's tough discipline, but it will keep you out of deep trouble.

Have you ever wondered how certain people can afford so much on what you assume are modest salaries? Watch their eyes, their body language. Are they always uptight, on edge? It's because they are living beyond their means, and if their bills were all called due in full, they'd be finished. If one of their kids fell seriously ill and their insurance covered only 80 percent of a whopping hospital bill, they'd be forced to look for charity. If they lost their jobs, they would have to take whatever was available as soon as possible, just to stay current with their debts.

Another problem with that kind of trap is that it's addictive. The more you have, the more you want. The more you have, the more you notice what others have. People get attention from fancy cars and the latest gadgets, and if that's more important to you than financial freedom, you'll make unwise purchases.

On the other hand, finding yourself among the 20 percent of Americans who live within their means will be wonderfully freeing. As your investments and savings accumulate, you'll be able to do things with your discretionary income that people mired in debt cannot. Your income and your spending and giving habits can then be just as much a part of your spiritual service of worship as your devotions and the sharing of your faith. Imagine how your dollars can be invested in lives and souls through ministries around the globe! Maybe you can afford to go on short-term missions trips if you make saving for that a priority.

A friend once asked for counsel about getting out from under a huge debt burden. Not being a financial wizard, I merely suggested a budget, sacrificing some entertainment and recreational dollars until the debt was retired. In the course of looking over his budget, I asked him to clarify whether he'd spent any more money recently that he hadn't listed.

"Well," he said, "we went shopping the other night, but we didn't spend any money."

I thought, *Good, we don't have to worry about that.*

But then he added, "We used credit cards."

People actually think like that. They believe that using credit cards is not spending money, when in fact it's worse than spending cash. It costs much more in the long run, and until my friend cut up his cards, he was never going to be free of their shackles. Ironically, he and his wife disciplined themselves to dig out of their debt hole, only to bury themselves again over the next year and a half. They used their freedom and borrowing power to buy more and more, and now both need to work full-time to stay afloat. It's no way to live.

Finally, I've saved one piece of counsel till last, but you'll recognize immediately that it is by no means the least important. Your first obligation, your first computation, should be what portion of your income you will designate specifically for God's work. There is wide debate among Christians on whether we are required by Scripture to tithe. I can't speak authoritatively on that, but I believe tithing is a minimum expectation.

As for the debate over whether we're to figure the percentage — whatever we come to — off our gross (before-tax) or net (after-tax) income, I'm much more confident. Don't take this as divine revelation, but to me it only makes sense that if we pay Caesar (or in our case the local, state, and federal governments) a percentage of our gross income, we should also figure God's portion from the same.

My counsel to you? Start at 10 percent of the gross of your base salary. If you find that after paying your bills and saving or investing you have extra money, tithe (or more) on that as well. Some people with significant incomes increase the percentage they give with every so many thousands of dollars they make. That's called spiral giving. Others give a certain percentage of their base salary and more from unexpected or extra income.

Whatever you decide upon will be pleasing to God if you're generous and, as Scripture points out, "cheerful" in your giving. "So let each one give as he purposes in his heart, not grudgingly or of necessity; for God loves a cheerful giver."[3]

The bottom line? (I just had to use that phrase in this chapter!) Avoid credit debt. Save and invest. Be conservative and frugal. Don't become an SFN addict. Give cheerfully. In doing these things, you will set yourself far apart from the crowd.

nine. on fitness, health, and nutrition

i have come late in life to this matter of fitness. The newly converted are always a bit obnoxious, so forgive me. Before I get into the spiritual and scriptural reasons to treat your body right, let me say this from a totally human perspective: It feels great! To be at the proper weight, to have the proper percentage of body fat, and to have cholesterol, blood pressure, and blood-sugar levels where they belong is like getting a new lease on life.

That's impossible to identify with at your age, perhaps, and I confess shame and regret for the years I neglected doing the right things. You can avoid that remorse by planning ahead. You may suffer less from a fast-food burger than someone of my vintage might, but even if you don't gain weight or look or feel any different, you may be building into your body cholesterol and fat levels that will eventually catch up with you.

It's hard to worry about such things—they sound so much like old people's concerns—when you're in the bloom of youth. But when you see men and women of the older generation who are trim and have vitality, make it your goal to maintain your fitness like them. I want you to do that for the glory of God, of course. But you might also do it for a selfish reason: Life is more fun that way. It's easier, less of a strain. You can be active for many years in all the physical pursuits you now enjoy if you take care of your body.

I know the apostle Paul told Timothy that bodily exercise profits little,[1] but be careful of the context. In that letter he was clearly warning against emphasizing the physical over the spiritual. Obviously, a healthy body with an unregenerate spirit will wind up in hell.

But it was also Paul who reminded the Corinthians that their bodies were the temples of the Holy Spirit.[2] Admittedly, his context there had to do with refraining from sexual immorality, but certainly other applications are valid. If our bodies are temples of the Holy Spirit, it only makes sense that we treat them well.

Paul also wrote, "I discipline my body and bring it into subjection, lest, when I have preached to others, I myself should become disqualified."[3] And, "You were bought at a price; therefore glorify God in your body and in your spirit, which are God's."[4]

Probably the most magnificent verses on this subject (not surprisingly, also penned by Paul) are, "According to my earnest expectation and hope that in nothing I shall be ashamed, but that with all boldness, as always, so now also Christ will be magnified in my body, whether by life or by death. For to me, to live is Christ, and to die is gain."[5]

Assuming you need no more evidence that our bodies are worthy of attention, so what? Spoken like a true young adult. How well I remember. I don't claim to be a nutritionist any more than I'm a financial wizard, but here come some basics in my last volley of advice on the subject before you're out of earshot.

You may have heard of the freshman 15. Those are the pounds college freshmen are alleged to put on as soon as they get out from under their families' watchful eyes and begin chowing down on fat-laden cafeteria food. I need to tell you something. Fifteen is an understatement, a kind way of saying what frequently happens to a 100-pound, or lighter, freshman girl. Bigger girls and much bigger guys increase at the same ratio, and that can mean a lot more than 15 pounds.

But is it only the difference in food that causes the weight gain? Of course not. Unless there's some severe physical or emotional problem that results in a true eating disorder, people gain weight by consuming more calories than they burn. That's it. Any fad, liquid, grapefruit, fast, protein, carbohydrate, store-front, chain, doctor-monitored, fat-free, low-sodium, diabetic, or other form of diet is based on that principle. They might each have a different wrinkle, and each may help people drop pounds, but only if those people consume fewer calories than they burn.

So what's happening to those freshmen? It could be anything. They might be eating more because it's available and they paid for it. They might be snacking all day and all night besides eating at meal times because it's a social thing. Maybe they're using junk food to substitute for the loss of their loved ones, anesthetizing themselves against homesickness. Even more significantly, and more likely, their level of physical activity has plunged. From daily gym classes and maybe vigorous varsity or intramural sports— not to mention romping with their friends in pickup basketball, football, softball, and so on—they have settled into a much more sedentary routine. They may be up more and sleeping less, but they're not burning a lot of calories sitting at a computer or in a library.

Now is when you will learn what so many middle-aged people have already: Unless you're somehow being forced into daily physical workouts, you have to discipline yourself. To lose weight, you must choose between fewer calories eaten or more calories burned. And unless you're a bricklayer, a P.E. coach, or an athlete, you'll have to force yourself to log some time, nearly every day, at some serious physical exertion. The time to do it is now, before the weight starts to creep up, because once it does, exercise appears more foreboding than it is.

Many experts will tell you that the best time to exercise is first thing in the morning, before you've eaten. If you work out correctly, you'll increase your metabolism for hours, which will help you digest and process your food more efficiently. Proper exercise is also an appetite suppressant. The reason I emphasize *proper* is that the right kind of workout is also excellent for your heart.

I know heart trouble is the last thing a young person worries about. Kids who gorge on greasy, fast-food burgers every day and never gain a pound wonder what all the fuss is about. But as I've said, even before you hit the sedentary life-style that brings on the hated pounds, you're building a base for cholesterol and other circulatory problems that can kill you, even if you're not overweight. Many people undergo heart bypass surgery though they never smoked, drank, or were heavy.

Dietitians recommend that we limit our fat intake to 30 percent or less of our total calories each day. (If you're already cringing because this seems to be getting too technical, stay with me. If I can get it, you can get it, and it's important.) Let's say you're happy with your weight. Multiply your weight by 12, and that's the number of calories you should be able to handle each day without gaining. If you gain, try 11 as your multiplier; if you drop weight and don't want to, try 13. If you overeat one day, cut back the next and it will even out. (When I got to the point where I owed myself seven years worth of cutback days, I knew it was time to get serious about my diet!)

Now, how do you figure fat percentages? It's easier than you might think. If you have your daily calorie intake figure, you can allow yourself up to 30 percent of those calories from fat. Most foods list fat content on the labels, but beware! For some reason, maybe to get you to buy their products despite their high fat content, food packagers list fat in grams, not calories. That means more work for you, but again, it's not that complicated.

Let's say you're looking at a product that's 150 calories to the ounce, and you want to eat one ounce. You will be thrilled to see that the fat content is only eight grams unless you know that every gram of fat equals nine calories. Ergo, the fat content in your food in question is eight times nine, or 72 of the 150 calories. You don't need to be a math whiz to know that's close to 50 percent of the total.

Don't despair. You can still enjoy that treat if the rest of the stuff you eat that day has significantly lower fat content. Don't assume you can never again indulge in something really outrageous. Work it into your total program, give yourself permission, and enjoy it. (Just remember that if you eat too much of the high-fat stuff, you'll have to chew sawdust for breakfast and Styrofoam for lunch!)

To make all that figuring a little easier, multiply fat grams by ten to get a rough calorie count. Easier yet is to determine how many fat grams you're allowed per day and just keep track of those rather than multiplying, adding, or dividing to get their caloric equivalents. If you're on 2,000 calories a day and have decided to keep your fat intake to less than 30 percent, you'll want to keep your fat grams per day under 60. Something like butter or oil might be 100 percent fat but amounts to just a few grams a day. Generally, look for foods with low fat percentages and you won't have to keep a separate set of books for your food intake. If food becomes a major problem for you and you start to gain, however, keeping a food diary may be a necessary precaution.

If you want to eat more or keep your cardiovascular system in good shape, work out hard nearly every day. Work up to between half an hour and an hour at some form of exercise that gets your heartbeat into a range of 60 to 80 percent of its maximum capacity. That, too, is easily figured. Subtract your age from 220 and multiply that figure by 60 percent and 80 percent. Anywhere between those two is where your pulse should be for at least 20 minutes, three days a week. The more often you get it there and keep it there, the more weight you'll lose (or the more extra calories you may allow yourself). Once your body has spent the first few minutes burning carbohydrates—when your heart is in the target range—it will burn fat the rest of the time.

You'll feel great for more reasons than simply being in the minority. (You won't know many people who carve out a half hour or an hour a day to hone their bodies.) There are also endorphins released in the brain—so they tell me—that give you a natural high when you've exerted like that. I've proved it for myself. I went from seeing the very idea of exercise as an insurmountable cliff to where I'm now out of sorts if I don't get a vigorous workout six times a week. You feel great for the rest of the day. Working out first thing in the morning also eliminates the need for two showers a day unless you insist on sprucing up before you sweat.

What you need to know about types of exercise is fairly simple and straightforward, too. Few of the fun sports are aerobic enough for what you're after (weight management). That doesn't mean they don't burn calories and aren't good for you. They make a nice supplement to your three-days-a-week cardiovascular routine. But to get your pulse into the target range and keep it there, you need something that will exercise your major muscle groups (arms and legs) for extended periods. That means jogging, walking, swimming, rope jumping, exercycling, stepping machines, and the like. Anything that makes you exert yourself but also involves brief periods of rest is considered anaerobic. In other words, you're not getting enough oxygen into your muscles to give your heart the workout it needs.

A combination of aerobic and anaerobic exercise is good. Hit the exercycle for half an hour and later play racquetball, lift weights, or play softball or basketball. To keep the exercise machines from boring you to death, bring plenty of reading material for the bike, or set the stepper in front of the TV. Even better, work out with someone else. You tend to show off for each other and work harder, and the time goes more quickly.

Most important, regardless of how you feel, start slowly and gradually work up to full-length, strenuous workouts. If you hurt yourself, strain a muscle, or wear yourself out before you've given the program a chance, you'll be a dropout. There's nothing wrong with beginning with just ten or 15 minutes on an exercycle, or even just four or five minutes on a stepping machine.

You'll be amazed that by adding just a few minutes each week, you'll soon be up to well over half an hour on each apparatus. If you can't work out four or five times a week or stay on a machine up to an hour, just remember the formula above: For the sake of your cardiovascular system alone, you want your heart rate in the target zone for at least 20 minutes, three times a week. That's the minimum. Any more that you can do should be fun and profitable.

While friends get soft, gain weight, and have less energy and sparkle, you'll be in shape, attacking life, and honoring God with your body.

As for the fitness of your mind, your commitment to staying in the Word is the best thing you can do, but there is something else as well. I once heard a speaker recommend an occasional media fast. It sounded strange to me, and I wondered if it were possible. Could I really go somewhere and tune out the TV, radio, tape player, video machine—even the fax and phone? I could and I did, and I survived—and I was the better for it.

If at all possible, schedule such times. It takes work, planning, and commitment, and at first you'll feel as if you've lost touch with the planet.

You'll have no clue to what's going on in the news, politics, sports, entertainment, music, and so on. But soon you won't care, and getting back to the so-called civilized world of communication will be scary and a bit of a letdown. If nothing else, the media fast will adjust your priorities and let you view with renewed perspective the images and sounds that are hurled at your senses every day.

The Lord Himself said, "Be still, and know that I am God."[6]

those all-important choices

ten. select a career wisely

P roverbs, that wonderful book of the sayings of Solomon (who chose wisdom above all else he wanted from God), has much to say about our work. For instance, "In all labor there is profit."[1] Technological advances have made almost every career and endeavor easier, which has somehow resulted in lazier people. Why work harder than we need to? Why work at all if we can push a few buttons and see things happen? There is danger in that thinking, however. Solomon also said, "The desire of the slothful kills him, for his hands refuse to labor."[2]

I would be the last one to thumb my nose at gadgets that make work easier, but it seems clear from Scripture that we should use the extra time we enjoy for more work, not only for our own pleasure. Not that there's anything wrong with enjoying life, particularly leisure time. God has given us all things to enjoy. The key here, as in any area of discipline, is balance and priorities.

Somehow, with this advent of technology, we get abusers of the workday on both ends of the spectrum. On the low end are the ones Solomon warned about, the slothful. They will look for any way to avoid work. That's why we have welfare cheats; something designed to bail out the truly needy has been abused by some who have found ways around the system. Then the whole program is underfunded when the ones who need it most seek help.

The apostle Paul said, "If anyone will not work, neither shall he eat."[3] That, strong as it may sound, is what I wish for you. Primarily, of course, my confidence is that you have a strong work ethic. But should you choose to be lazy and live off someone else or off the system, I want you to fail. I want you to not be able to support yourself unless you work or are legitimately unable. That's why, even when financing your life or your education, I expect you to do your part. That's the way it is, and that's the way it should be.

On the other end of the spectrum are those who have overbalanced on the work side. They have seen the advent of fax machines, copy machines, overnight mail, satellite communications, answering machines, computers, and laser technology as the way to do much more work in much less time—but not so they can have time to regroup and recharge their batteries. They were workaholics before all this came along, putting in 12- to 16-hour days. Now they can do twice or three times as much, and if they can squeeze an extra hour or two into their workday, they can interact with international markets, too.

Their spiritual lives are gone. Their marriages are in trouble. Their interpersonal relationships are now based on a what's-in-it-for-me attitude. If you can't bring some benefit, some contact, some sale, or some influence to them, they don't have time for you. Many die young, knotted with hypertension, high cholesterol, heart trouble, depression, stress, and even substance abuse.

Believe it or not, Solomon actually had something to say about those types, too: "For what has man for all his labor, and for the striving of his heart with which he has toiled under the sun? For all his days are sorrowful, and his work grievous; even in the night his heart takes no rest. This also is vanity."[4]

There has to be a happy medium, and you can spend a lifetime trying to find it. That's not a bad pursuit. Find a vocation that challenges you, keeps you learning, excites you, rewards you. Use every modern convenience to help you do it the best way you know how, to the glory of God. "And whatever you do, do it heartily, as to the Lord and not to men, knowing that from the Lord you will receive the reward of the inheritance; for you serve the Lord Christ."[5]

What a freeing thought that is! We serve the Lord Christ whether we're in secular work or full-time Christian service. The answer to the question "What do you do?" should then be, "I'm a servant of the Lord Christ." Of course, you want to be careful to whom you say that. If the people are outside the faith, they might think you're off your nut. But it's true, isn't it, that Christian workers in secular situations ought to be the most valuable, most trusted employees around. They (including you) should be prompt, thorough, cooperative, productive, and teachable.

The big question is how someone decides what to pursue for a career. Some kids know from childhood precisely what they want to do. They never waver in following their dreams. Once you've outgrown wanting to be an astronaut, a firefighter, or a ballet dancer, you might panic, wondering how to know which way to go. I recommend taking advantage of every personality profile test available. Some of them may seem like hocus-pocus, and others have fallen into disrepute with employers because they relied too heavily on them in choosing workers. But there is still benefit in getting all the input you can about your own preferences. Take advantage of career days, job marts, and recruiters.

Most important: If at all possible, make a career out of what you love to do and do well. If you don't love it and it becomes your life, you won't love your life. If you don't do well at it, you'll struggle.

That may be oversimplified, but you'd be amazed at the people who should be in sales because of their personalities, yet they get into management for some prestige motive and are miserable for years. And some born teachers are in sales for the money. Stories of misfit personalities abound.

One expert wrote a whole book on the theme "Do what you love and the money will follow." The point was that if you love something enough, you'll pour your passion and life into it, and success will naturally follow. To that I would add that you need to beware investing your entire self-image in your career. In this age when loyal employees lose their jobs every day, your whole sense of self-worth can come crashing down when you find yourself unemployed. Your identity and worth are in Christ. Your job is not who you are; it's only what you do.

I can guarantee you this, after years in the work force: If you merely do your job, you'll stick out like a sore thumb. Sure, there are many overachievers and workaholics. But there are many more people who see their jobs as merely time spent to get a paycheck. They either do what they're told or try to avoid being told anything by looking busy all the time and accomplishing little.

Do your job. When a task is finished, look or ask for something more to do. You won't feel so special or so accomplished, but you will skyrocket to more responsibility. I'm telling you, the work force is generally so lazy and so interested in avoiding work that the man or woman who merely fulfills the job description will look like a star.

Then, know when to quit. When you're new on a job, that's not the time to put limits on yourself. Yes, you may have to work a lot of extra hours, proving yourself, learning new things. But once you've become comfortable and efficient, you need to decide how productive you should be in relation to the other priorities in your life. Will you allow your job to take precedence over your spiritual growth, your spouse, your children?

What about your down time? While competitors for high-level positions contend to see who can get to the office first and stay the longest, will you be sucked into that game? If you're working only for riches or ego strokes, you are no longer doing your job as a servant of Christ. You're serving money, and you cannot serve two masters. One will have to fade. I pray it is not the One to whom your service belongs.

Transiency is an epidemic in the job market today. People are constantly moving, shifting, trying to better themselves. Loyalty to a company—and, yes, *from* a company—is becoming more and more rare. Some people job hop every year or two, leaving an expensive trail of training that may have set them up to succeed but which has been nothing but a costly headache for the employers who made them what they are.

The résumés of such people look like road maps, and when the truly interesting and choice openings come along, companies look for better risks, longer-term people, those who have proved their loyalty and their ability to stick with an organization.

That's a good reason to do your job hopping and shopping early. It's not a major issue if you've moved two or three times before you're 25. But then it's time to find your niche. Discover the vocation that reaches you, that makes you eager to get up in the morning and get back at it. Few people are more miserable than those who find themselves mired in jobs they hate. They've reached a certain age or income level that makes it nearly impossible to change, and there they sit for the rest of their lives. They resent the commute, they don't like their bosses, they dislike their tasks. The thing in their lives that consumes more of their time than anything else is the most distasteful. That's no way to live.

So choose with care. Go prayerfully into your search for the right position and situation. And be prepared to decide early whether you want a career and a paycheck to dominate your life, because if you do, you'd be better off to forget about a spouse and family. Obviously, that would not be my wish for you, because you would miss out on the kind of wonder and joy you have brought to me and our family.

Suffice it to say that if you give your employer the appropriate time and productivity to earn your income, you should have enough time for relaxing, for family time, for recreation, for staying healthy, for remaining a rounded person. That will make you a better employee, too, and most employers are beginning to see that.

If someone less qualified but more committed to long hours passes you on the way up the corporate ladder, wave as he goes by. You may just wave again when he falls and flies past you on the way down someday. "He who trusts in his riches will fall, but the righteous will flourish like foliage."[6]

Your career choice will determine how much time you'll be able to spend with your loved ones. By now you've heard more than one speaker or many more than one writer say that no one, on his deathbed, ever said he wished he'd spent more time at the office. And those people who bought into the quality-time-versus-quantity-time myth have long since discovered its folly.

If that's new to you, it goes like this: "I'm so busy that I don't have much time for my family, but the time I do spend with them is quality time." What drivel! As if children know the difference! Kids don't want to discuss the meaning of the cosmos every time they get a few minutes with a parent. They might simply want to wrestle with you or climb you. They might even want to ignore you and simply be assured that you're there for them.

Nothing will more determine your priorities than what you decide to do with the major portion of your time. Your personal spiritual life, church life, family life, health—everything will be hung on that framework. Be sure the job is worth the time, worth the trip, worth the investment of your life.

One thing you should know by now: If you become famous, a star, a wealthy person who can afford every gadget available, I'll be proud of you. But that's not what I covet for you, especially if that's your goal. If your goal is to serve Christ and all those things happen to come as by-products, good for you. But if your devotion to God takes you halfway around the world to where you will live with no indoor plumbing and no car, let alone two or three, you couldn't thrill me more.

"For where your treasure is, there your heart will be also."[7]

eleven. select friends even more wisely

ou can protect yourself against being hurt by never opening your heart to anyone. In doing that, however, you'll miss out on one of life's great fortunes. Good friends can be sources of joy and companionship, communication and fun, accountability and discipleship. As important as it is to avoid running with the wrong crowd, it's equally critical to draw to yourself those select few friends who will bring out the best in you, and vice versa. Some call these your five-finger friends (those you can count on the fingers of one hand). If you even get near having five such friends in your lifetime, consider yourself richly blessed.

How do you determine whether people fit that category? First, they must share your faith. That doesn't mean you agree with them on every jot and tittle of doctrine and practice. In fact, it's especially stimulating to enjoy the company of someone who brings another perspective to your spiritual journey. On the basics, however, you must agree. For when one of you loses a loved one or health or wealth, or when you go through waters so deep that none but your five-finger friends will stay with you, that's not the time to be arguing over the bedrock principles of the faith.

Make no mistake, friends outside the faith can be as loving and honest (sometimes more) with you than your Christian friends. I would never advise you to shun them or eliminate them from your orbit. You can learn much from such people, and of course you may have an influence on them for God. But in my mind, your short list of best friends will be your siblings in Christ.

Who will make the cut? (I don't mean that to sound as if you'll audition and qualify those you choose to call close friends.) If your experience is like mine, your five-finger friends will surprise you over the years. They won't necessarily be the friends you most enjoy now. They won't be the funniest, the most fun-loving, or the most popular, talented, or attractive of your acquaintances. (Sometimes in our youth or immaturity, we think such qualities in our buddies make us look good.)

No, these will be people who quietly emerge to stand the test of time. Your five-finger friends will be the ones who step forward to serve without reward, to be there when you really need them without being asked, to be honest with you when you might rather they not be—only to look back and appreciate that risky a love.

I urge you to limit your five-finger friends to your same sex, no matter how someone else might click with you or how you resonate with an individual. Of course, your spouse should be your very best friend, and the intimacy you two will share should go far beyond my definition here.

If you're still having trouble getting a handle on the type of person I'm talking about, ask yourself this: Will the person you're thinking about want to be among the first to know when you decide to marry the love of your life? When you have a child? When you endure a tragedy? When you celebrate a significant joy? Would he or she stand by you in a time of crisis, no questions asked? Would he or she be offended to know that you endured something without letting him or her know? Believe it or not, that offense is a sign of true friendship. A real friend deserves to know when you've failed, when you're feeling vulnerable, and when you're hanging by your fingernails, because that friend has invested emotionally in you.

A bedrock question when considering five-finger friends: Will that person attend your funeral? Would you attend his, letting nothing, save impossibilities, keep you from somehow getting there?

A friend I thought was just a fun guy spent a few weeks in the hospital some years ago. He had medium-serious surgery, not life-threatening but dangerous. As I puzzled over why he should constantly come to mind and why I should be drawn not just to call or send a card but also to go see him a good hour away, it came to me. Over the years, through work relationships and lots of fun social times, we had become deep friends, trusted brothers. We shared our real selves at gut level, almost without realizing it.

We might go weeks at a time without connecting, yet when we got back together, we picked up again right where we had left off. As I thought of him in the hospital, stitched up from the surgery and feeling that particular puniness that comes from the trauma of an operation, I imagined myself in his shoes.

Would I have expected him to visit me? Possibly not. Did he expect me to visit him? I sincerely doubt it. Our friendship would not have suffered if I had not. But again, trying to think as he would think, I asked myself how I would respond if I were laid up and he came. I would be thrilled. It would make a statement to me. It would cement our relationship.

Make no mistake, my going was no great virtue or sacrifice. And I certainly wasn't trying to make some dramatic, maudlin declaration. I made no pronouncements, didn't wax eloquent, didn't milk any grand, effusive thanks for taking the time. I just went because I realized he was a five-finger friend. And since then we have consciously been that type of friend to each other.

We don't talk about it or make a big deal of it. I just know he'll be there for me when I need him, and he knows the same about me. Also on my short list is a relative I chanced to spend some uninterrupted time with a few years ago. Besides the commonality of having married into the same family, we discovered basic philosophical agreements. This has proved to be a long-distance, hit-and-miss relationship, and we joke that if it were less distant and more frequent, we might discover we can't stand each other.

Also on my short list is a dear brother in Christ who is half a generation older than I and who has preceded me through life's stages—kids growing up and leaving, getting married, having their own children. Somehow, despite the difference in age, we hit it off and keep in touch. You don't know how these things happen. You can't predict them. But you must be open and prepared.

A rare treasure on your five-finger list is a friendship that lasts a lifetime. One who has been a friend for decades cannot be replaced. When you're in each other's weddings, see each other's children born, vacation together, enjoy all-night gabfests, let your hair down, and enjoy the privilege of being drop-dead honest with each other—and suffer the pain when you aren't—that all becomes part of the mosaic of your life. True short-list friends know all about you and love you just the same. When they think you're wrong, they either say so or give you the benefit of the doubt. The best part about long-term friends is that they don't just hear about your past; they're part of it. That makes the relationship worth preserving.

By now I shouldn't have to warn you against so-called friends who would drag you down. They're the type who are fun and funny, exciting and wild, "really, really nice," but simply not good for you in the long run. They're the types you may need to befriend and maintain relationships with so you can witness to them. But they're not your five-finger friends. If you find yourself less consistent and disciplined when you're with them, less likely to do what you know is right and to abstain from what you know is wrong, that's more than a clue. That's a trumpet blast. Maintain, maintain, maintain. Without preaching, without condescension, you must carefully separate yourself from bad influences, and you know who they are. Unless you're some super saint, their negative influence will almost always overcome your positive.

What about friends who call themselves Christians yet live in open defiance of the Bible? This is a tough one, but Scripture is clear. In an interesting passage, the apostle Paul wrote to the Corinthians that they should not keep company with sexually immoral people. He quickly clarified that he didn't mean the sexually immoral people "of this world, or with the covetous, or extortioners, or idolaters." If we were to separate ourselves from all such people, we would need to leave the world entirely. But Paul went on to exhort the Corinthians—and us, of course—to not "keep company with anyone *named a brother*, who is a fornicator, or covetous, or an idolater, or a reviler, or a drunkard, or an extortioner; not even to eat with such a person. For what have I to do with judging those also who are *outside*? Do you not judge those who are *inside*?" (italics added).[1]

So, that unmarried couple who wants to visit you and sleep together? If they're Christians, you have to initiate a difficult confrontation. The friend who calls himself a Christian but gets drunk or sleeps around? It's hard to argue with the above Scripture. Yet Paul made an excellent side point about non-Christians who do the same. He asked what business it is of ours to judge those who are outside the church or the faith. That doesn't mean we condone their actions. It certainly doesn't mean we join them. Neither does it mean we don't, when appropriate, make clear that theirs is not an acceptable life-style for us. But they don't claim to live by the standards of the Bible. Without looking down our noses at them, we're to love them, accept them (but not their actions), and maintain a relationship that will allow us to influence them for Christ.

If you maintain a consistent witness before carousing, impure friends, the day will come when they're vulnerable. When life has caught up with them and they're past fixing things on their own, they will remember which of their friends had a bedrock peace, which one had something they wished they had in their lives.

You'll be afraid to confront Christian friends who flout the tenets of Scripture if you share a common misunderstanding and misapplication of a famous passage that quotes Jesus Himself: "Judge not, that you be not judged. For with what judgment you judge, you will be judged; and with the same measure you use, it will be measured back to you."[2]

That doesn't mean that neither you nor your Christian friends have a right to say anything to each other about what you choose to do. Under the guise of love and respect and remaining nonjudgmental, we too often look the other way when a brother or sister is clearly living immorally. And then we spout, "Judge not!"

If someone is living in open sin, there is no judgment call to be made. Even Paul said, "Do you not judge those who are inside?"[3]

Obviously, we don't want our churches and Christian social groups to become God-squadders, running around with clipboards and checking off who's naughty and nice. But purity is expected within the Body. We're to maintain our witness before unsaved acquaintances who do not live for God, but we're to separate ourselves from immoral brothers and sisters in Christ who don't respond to exhortation and admonition.

That's a difficult thing to do. It seems judgmental and unloving. When someone has been disciplined by a church and has been separated from the body of believers, there will always be those who decide the punishment is too severe. Before repentance and restoration have occurred, they take it upon themselves to maintain contact and support the offending party. Scripture makes clear that this threatens the integrity of the church and defiles the reputation of Christ.

Separating ourselves from believers living in open sin is an ugly, distasteful business, and we can easily say, "Hey, I'm not much better. There, but for the grace of God, go I." We never want to set ourselves up as paragons of virtue, but we do need to take seriously the scriptural admonition that people who call themselves followers of Christ cannot simply flout His standards.

So don't cut yourself off from the world or you'll never know the joy of leading someone to Christ.

Be careful of the influence non-Christian friends have on you and your conduct.

Take the high road with believers who are living in sin.

And stay open to special, five-finger relationships that will enrich your life.

twelve. select a mate most wisely of all

Second to receiving Christ, your choice of a lifetime partner is the most significant decision you will ever make. There's no substitute for God's part in the process; which of us has a clue to what member of the opposite sex will best suit us for the rest of our lives?

Everything wars against the success of marriages these days. Divorce, even in the church, has become so common that, for many, there is hardly a stigma to it anymore. The embarrassment of a divorce should not in itself be the primary reason to stay together. But with splits so common, more ministries for divorced people are springing up than for people who are trying to make their marriages work.

Ministering to people in pain from broken marriages is good, of course. But the only way to ensure better, longer-lasting unions is to somehow do better things on the front end.

A good marriage is very much of God. There has to be the spark of the divine in the miracle of disparate personalities, sexes, backgrounds, and egos meshing for the benefit of each other, their eventual family, and Christ and His church. When couples know each other for between just six and 24 months before they wed, it's a wonder they can build a relationship that would last a lifetime.

Obviously, you're looking for a Christian who shares your views on the major doctrines of Scripture. Love may overcome minor differences in your church backgrounds, but there will be enough things to work out in other areas of your lives that you should not to try to force together two widely dissimilar cultures. I'm speaking more here of religious environment than even of racial or socioeconomic. Though I see no biblical prohibition against weddings between people of different races or nationalities (and indeed am aware of God-honoring cross-cultural marriages), those, too, are challenges that should not be entered into lightly.

The more of the basics of faith and practice you agree on, the less you'll have to haggle over later. That becomes more important when you have children. You can disagree harmlessly over many things without threatening your relationship, but your kids will look to you for unity and strength.

If there is one bit of advice more important than the rest in considering a spouse, it's this: You should determine early, above all else, that *divorce* will have no place in your vocabulary. If either of you is not rigid on that, beware. I'm not suggesting that anyone should be expected to live in a life-threatening situation, but surely if either partner had the remotest inkling of that eventuality, they wouldn't consider marriage in the first place.

When you're thinking about spending the rest of your lives together, you're usually so head over heels in love that you ignore weaknesses, foibles, differences, and idiosyncrasies. Those may become major irritations in the months and years to come, but they're nothing that should jeopardize the future of the marriage. Too often, people not committed to the sanctity and permanence of marriage find themselves letting the "D" word into their conversation and arguments. Before you know it, they're seriously considering splitting.

Eccentricities and peculiarities you find charming in your courtship might drive you crazy one day, but if divorce is not part of your vocabulary, you'll learn to work through those things or even laugh them off. How much

125

better to enjoy the differences and see the humor in them than to go berserk trying to change your partner! While marriage experts disagree on many things, they all agree on this: You must accept, accept, accept and give, give, give. Why should your spouse be just like you, even if your way is better? Maybe you're neater or quieter or more sensitive. On the other hand, your partner may be more articulate, harder working, or have more endurance. One of you will be more patient; one more prompt. If you want to improve in an area your mate excels at, fine. That's your choice. But don't expect to whip another human being into shape, especially over nonessentials.

Two of the things I learned in marriage, as a direct result of seeing these attributes modeled every day, are politeness and promptness. It isn't that those were absent from my character before, but I was neither as well-mannered at home nor as punctual in any venue as I should have been.

Dianna never mentioned either of those differences to me or even made a face about them. I was not nagged, harped on, or badgered. Had I been, my flesh would likely have rebelled. I don't say that as a defense, nor am I proud of that, but it likely would have taken me much longer to become aware and change.

But by seeing a daily model of manners and politeness even simply at home, where "please" and "thank you" and "you're welcome" were as natural a part of her speech as anything, I learned by osmosis. And while the stereotypical husband is always waiting on his chronically late, primping wife (usually because she has been left with the chore of getting the kids ready, too), I quickly became aware that my wife was never, ever late. What a benefit to me! I grew obsessive about promptness and can see that better manners and timeliness are direct benefits of my marriage. So, be willing to learn and change yourself, but not to teach and change your mate.

Remember that love is an act of the will. It is not a state of being, something you're in rather than what you do. People say they've lost their love, fallen out of love, no longer love, maybe never loved—all as rationalization for what went wrong in their marriages. Love is not something you can be in or out of unless you're talking about puppy love or infatuation. Real love is a decision, and it comes long after the initial rush has worn off.

What happens if you marry in the flower of infatuation and then that fades? I've seen couples discover that without the idealistic warm fuzzies still surrounding their fairy-tale love story, they actually don't like each other very much. What then? Weeks and months of pasted-on smiles and pretending to be happy in front of friends, neighbors, and relatives before becoming another divorce statistic? It need not be.

I also know of couples who decided their vows meant more to them than that. Perhaps they didn't know enough about each other before marrying, shouldn't have married so young, and got off on the wrong foot. Maybe they regretted their decision and the future looked bleak, waking up every morning next to someone they'd rather not be with. I can't imagine it personally, but it happens.

The same God who saved us while we were yet dead in our sins can rescue marriages that died because people were unaware that love is a verb. Love by doing, love by loving, love by serving. Acting out the love you promised to bestow can birth in your partner a strange, warm, wonderful reaction. It often will also awaken in you feelings of passion you thought were gone. The kingdom is replete with stories of love rekindled because, rather than giving up in despair, couples recommitted themselves to making it work—not because they had to, but because they wanted to. Often their new union, born of a more mature, truer love than they had ever known, becomes more idyllic than even what they thought they had before.

I'm one of those people who believes God is directly involved in people getting together as husband and wife. Many disagree with me on this, and frankly, their arguments are more logical than mine. I have a bit of an idealized view because I'm a romantic. I enjoy believing God created someone just for me and vice versa. I like tracing our paths until we met and seeing how God put us together, attracted us to each other, and helped us build a life.

Because our marriage has been so wonderful, I like to believe there could have been no one else for me and that had I made the wrong choice, I would have been miserable. That may not be the case, of course. Many godly people believe the Lord allows a variety of choices and that any one of several partners could have been virtually interchangeable. The problem with my view is that if you carry it to its logical, or illogical, conclusion, it could justify some craziness.

For instance, a former friend once told me that he had an affair, divorced his wife, broke up the marriage of his lover, and married her because he believed she had been God's choice for him from the beginning. He had, he said, made a mistake the first time around. He had ignored the leadings of the Spirit and married the wrong person, and now, ten years and a family later, he was making things right—by the affair, the divorce, and the remarriage. Of course, bringing God into it helped salve his conscience. Any rationalization would have done for his unconscionable behavior that wreaked havoc in many lives.

So, I don't offer my starry view of marriage as the definitive answer, and certainly not as an excuse for matrimonial bedlam until the right partner is struck upon. I do pray for you, however, that you keep your wits about you. Move carefully and cautiously along the path to this most momentous selection. Should you discover the person God selected for you from the beginning of time, you'll have a gigantic head start on staving off niggling problems that might otherwise seem insurmountable.

If you believe you were destined to be together, what could stand in the way of that? My mother prayed for my wife before I was born. Did you catch that? While I was still in my mother's womb, she prayed for the woman I would marry one day. She didn't know whether my wife-to-be was even born yet herself, but Mom prayed that my wife would be a godly woman of virtue, someone who would be the best partner I could find, and that I would be the same for her. What a precious thought!

That may be why, when we first met in our twenties, it seemed I had loved her all my life—even before I knew her. I'll never forget browsing through her family's photo albums and seeing her as a little girl, wondering where I was the moment each picture had been snapped. We had never heard of each other, knew nothing about each other, yet we believe our paths were inexorably pointed at one another.

May you enjoy such a love relationship and, if it's God's will, such a marriage! But should your future instead hold the possibility of a difficult, contentious relationship that would make you regret ever marrying, I pray the signs will be clear enough from the beginning that you'll be able to avoid the union before it starts. It would be a hundred times better to remain single than to endure a bad marriage or, worse, a divorce.

Because I'm in the flush of sentiment that helps me release you to discover life on your own, I foresee nothing but sunshine for you. I know better, and as I've said, I don't want your growth stunted or your character spoiled by your never having to build spiritual muscle during hard times. But I covet for you a marriage that will be part of the cure and not part of the ill of your life. Above all the other dreams and hopes I have for you, I would to God that you find deep, lasting, and faithful love that will bear you over any obstacle.

The greatest product of our love is you. You could enjoy no finer blessing than to have God produce children from your pure love relationship. You'll make mistakes with them. Your shortcomings will be magnified in them. You'll suffer anxiety and worry because of them. But they will also be the source of your greatest joy and hope.

You'll wonder at the majesty of the miracle when they burst from the womb, and you'll wonder if the sleepless nights will ever end. You'll nod politely when people tell you that tomorrow they'll be gone.

And suddenly you'll turn around one day and realize that the years have indeed slipped by faster than any well-intentioned adviser could have predicted. The baby had become a toddler, a preschooler, a kindergartner, a sixth-grader, an adolescent, a teenager. Seemingly instantaneously, despite all your efforts to hold on, to savor, to enjoy, the child has become a young adult for only the briefest flash.

While I can hardly dislodge from my mind the crystal-clear picture of that scrawny newborn, I can deny it no longer. Ready or not, here you come. I may not want to believe your grown-up body contains the independent mind of a fully-functioning adult, but I know better than to stand in your way and be the reason the world doesn't find out.

I realize we won't become strangers. As I fight the feeling that one more embrace will be our last ever—and thus I would never let go—I wish you God's speed. I wish you His best. I wish you the knowledge that you go with the deepest love a parent can have for a child. You will have no greater cheerleader in the game of life.

notes

chapter one

1. James 4:14

2. From "We Have This Moment, Today," by William J. and Gloria Gaither. Copyright 1975 by William J. Gaither. International copyright secured. All rights reserved.

3. From "I Wish You." Words by Gloria Gaither. Music by William J. Gaither. Copyright 1977 by William J. Gaither. International copyright secured. All rights reserved.

4. Ephesians 2:4-5

chapter two

1. See Job 5:7

2. Job 5:8-9

3. 1 John 3:20

4. Public domain

chapter three

1. See John 14:6

2. See Ephesians 2:4-5

3. 1 Samuel 16:7*b*

chapter four
1. Ephesians 4:26
2. Hebrews 10:30
3. Romans 8:11
4. James 4:14
5. Luke 12:15-21

chapter five
1. Matthew 18:15

chapter six
1. 1 Corinthians 10:13
2. 1 Thessalonians 5:17
3. See Psalm 61:8
4. See Psalm 68:19
5. Psalm 72:15
6. Isaiah 58:2
7. See 1 Corinthians 15:31
8. See John 3:30
9. Hebrews 10:25

chapter seven

1. 1 Thessalonians 4:3,7
2. Romans 12:2
3. 1 Peter 2:15
4. 1 John 2:17
5. 1 Corinthians 1:27
6. 2 Timothy 2:22

chapter eight

1. 1 Timothy 6:10
2. Ron and Judy Blue, A *Woman's Guide to Financial Peace of Mind* (Pomona, Calif.: Focus on the Family, 1991), p. 57.
3. 2 Corinthians 9:7

chapter nine

1. See 1 Timothy 4:8
2. See 1 Corinthians 6:19
3. 1 Corinthians 9:27
4. 1 Corinthians 6:20
5. Philippians 1:20-21
6. Psalm 46:10

chapter ten

1. Proverbs 14:23*a*
2. Proverbs 21:25
3. 2 Thessalonians 3:10
4. Ecclesiastes 2:22-23
5. Colossians 3:23-24
6. Proverbs 11:28
7. Luke 12:34

chapter eleven

1. 1 Corinthians 5:9-12
2. Matthew 7:1-2
3. 1 Corinthians 5:12